CULTURES OF THE WORLD
Canada

Cavendish
Square

New York

Published in 2015 by Cavendish Square Publishing, LLC
243 5th Avenue, Suite 136, New York, NY 10016

Library of Congress Cataloging-in-Publication Data

Pang, Guek-Cheng.
Canada / by Guek-Cheng Pang, Jo-Ann Spilling, and Deborah Nevins.
    p. cm. — (Cultures of the world)
 Includes index.
 ISBN 978-0-76144-991-1 (hardcover) — ISBN 978-0-76147-991-8 (ebook)
1. Canada — Juvenile literature. I. Pang, Guek-Cheng, 1950-. II. Title.
 F1008.2 .C44 2015
 971—d23

Writers, Guek-Cheng Pang; Deborah Nevins, third edition
Editorial Director, third edition: Dean Miller
Editor, third edition: Deborah Nevins
Art Director, third edition: Jeffrey Talbot
Designer, third edition: Jessica Nevins
Production Manager, third edition Jennifer Ryder-Talbot
Production Editors: Andrew Coddington and David McNamara
Picture Researcher, third edition: Jessica Nevins

Printed in the United States of America

CONTENTS

CANADA TODAY

ARE CANADIANS THE HAPPIEST PEOPLE ON EARTH? According to the Legatum Institute, which issues a yearly Prosperity Index, the answer is a resounding yes. In 2013, Canada ranked third in the world, behind only Norway and Switzerland, in such categories as personal freedom, education, economy, governance, health, and safety.

In a different survey, the 2013 World Happiness Report, issued by the United Nations Sustainable Development Network, Canada came in sixth out of 156. This index considered factors such as life expectancy, personal freedom, social support, freedom from corruption, and generosity.

Lovely weather is obviously not a criterion for happiness in either case, since the top countries on both lists include wintery Sweden, Norway, Denmark, and Switzerland. And of course, Canada—nicknamed the Great White North—is also not known for its sultry climate. In general, the qualities that the happiest countries share are peace and freedom, quality healthcare and education, a stable, functioning government, and opportunity. That seems an apt description of Canada.

At the famous Calgary Stampede, a summer festival, an amusement park is part of the fun.

Naturally, trying to quantify happiness is an exercise in futility. Such surveys are overviews of societies, and not indicative of individuals. After all, in Canada, as in any country, there are people who are perfectly happy and those who are perfectly miserable. Most people fall somewhere in between. Nevertheless, Canada is a pretty good place, and Canadians— or Canucks as they are popularly called—tend to agree.

Canadians enjoy a mostly friendly relationship with their superpower neighbor to the south. The United States is Canada's only neighbor, making Canada the largest country in the world that borders only one country. The two countries share a border of 5,525 miles (8,892 km), including the Alaska-Canada border.

Stereotypes run both ways across the border. Canadians will point out that the relationship between the two countries is a bit lopsided. While Canadians are interested in U.S. news, are generally knowledgeable about the country, and could certainly name the U.S. president, the reverse is far from true. Some Canucks grouse that most Americans probably couldn't find Canada on a map, never mind name the prime minister. Indeed, in 2012, all three contestants on an episode of the U.S. game show *Jeopardy* failed to name Stephen Harper as Canada's prime minister.

Americans, for their part, tend to view their northern neighbor as pleasant but somewhat boring. They joke that Canada is America's hat. Others see Canada as a kind of escape valve if things in the U.S. get out of hand. (In fact, during the Vietnam War years, the 1960s and early '70s, about 125,000 young American men fled to Canada to avoid being drafted into the military.)

Some Americans think of Canada as being "the United States, but

better"—a greener, more progressive nation with a positive standing in the world, better healthcare, and lower crime; a peaceful land of toque-wearing lumberjacks, grizzly bears, moose, Eskimos, and hockey nuts. Indeed the worst violence in Canada can seem to take place on the hockey rink.

In general, the world looks kindly on Canada. But then there's the country's annual seal hunt—or, some would say, its inhumane slaughter of baby seals. In the spring, harp seals give birth to pups on the ice floes off the Canadian Atlantic coastline of Newfoundland and Labrador and in the Gulf of St. Lawrence to the east of Quebec. The pups' fur is soft and snowy white and valued by the fur industry. During the hunt, local men go out on the ice floes and club the pups to death.

Critics claim the slaughter inflicts great pain and suffering on the animals. Outrage over the process pours in from around the globe. Defenders of the hunt point out that the seal pelts provide livelihoods for people in remote areas where few other opportunities exist. Native peoples have hunted seals for centuries, they say. Indigenous people killed adult seals for their

A baby harp seal pup enjoys the sun on an ice floe.

Anti-fracking protesters hold a rally in Vancouver.

fur, meat, and bones, which were used for food, clothing, and shelter. These animals were valued for contributing to their survival. The modern hunt is no different, they say, but many disagree.

Canada has other hot-button issues as well. The country's powerful energy industries are at the center of some of them. For example, *fracking*, or hydraulic fracturing, a method of obtaining natural gas, is controversial. It involves drilling deep into the ground and using fluid under pressure to fracture shale rock to release the natural gas trapped in the rock. Critics argue that the process permanently damages the landscape and releases toxic materials into the soil, water, and air. UNESCO, the United Nations entity that identifies the world's cultural and natural treasures, has threatened to revoke the World Heritage site designation of the majestic Gros Morne National Park in Newfoundland and Labrador. The reason? Nearby fracking activities could damage the site's geological structure.

The Keystone Pipeline is another area of environmental conflict. The oil pipeline, owned by TransCanada Corp., starts in the province of Alberta, where Canada's greatest oil resources are located. The pipeline brings oil to refineries in the United States in Nebraska, Illinois, and the Gulf Coast of Texas. The first three parts of the project have been completed, but the fourth and last part is causing controversy. Phase IV, Keystone XL, is to run from Alberta to Steele City, Nebraska, replacing the old Phase I portion of the line. Protesters say the line would run through environmentally sensitive regions. They voice concern about oil leaks and other forms of pollution damaging to wildlife, wetland ecosystems, and aquifers (underground water sources). To the consternation of Canada's oil industry and many politicians, the project is on hold amid heated debate in the United States.

Conflicts aside, however, Canucks have a positive, forward-looking attitude. They celebrate their diverse population, cosmopolitan cities, awe-inspiring natural landscapes, progressive social programs, arts and culture, industry—and of course, hockey. In 2017, they will celebrate their 150th birthday as a country—and what better way to party than with a big plate of poutine, some sugar pie, schmoo cake, butter tarts, and a rousing chorus of "O Canada"!

Time lapse photography captures national pride in sparklers as part of a Canada Day (July 1) celebration.

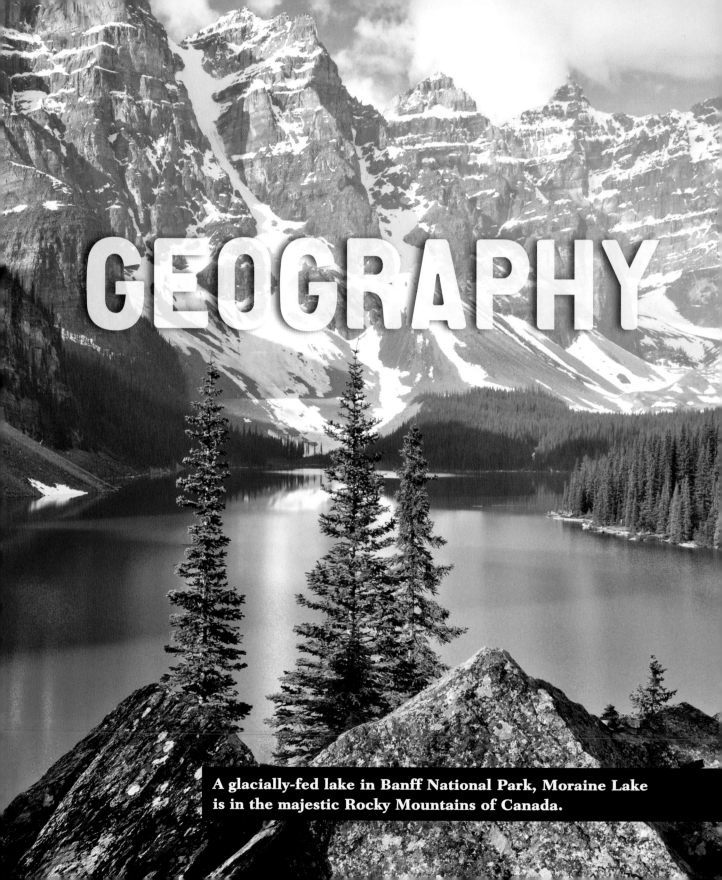

GEOGRAPHY

A glacially-fed lake in Banff National Park, Moraine Lake is in the majestic Rocky Mountains of Canada.

1

CANADA ISN'T THE EASIEST COUNTRY to draw on paper. Unlike ladle-shaped Norway, boot-like Italy, or chicken-shaped China, Canada doesn't resemble anything in particular. And unlike many countries, such as France or even the United States, it isn't a relatively nice, neat shape. Canadian schoolchildren don't have an easy task when it comes to drawing a map of their homeland, because its jagged coastlines and multitude of islands make Canada look like a jigsaw puzzle that has fallen apart. Not only that, but it's a puzzle with a huge piece missing smack in the middle of it. That's Hudson Bay.

But Canada isn't falling apart at all. In fact, it's a very "together" country, so to speak, a country that is mostly at peace within its borders as well as beyond them; an excellent citizen of the world. It's the second-largest country on Earth. Its land area totals more than 3.8 million square miles (9.8 million square km). Only Russia is bigger than Canada. Despite its size, Canada is a benevolent and even modest giant. Perhaps that's because it is also one of the most sparsely populated countries in the

The border between Canada and the United States is officially known as the International Boundary. At 5,525 miles (8,892 km.) long, including 1,538 miles (2,475 km) between Canada and Alaska, it is the world's longest border between two nations.

A spectacular display of Northern Lights, or Aurora borealis, forms green swirls over a snowy landscape.

world, with much of its land located in the frozen north. Approximately 90 percent of Canadians live within 100 miles (160 km) of the U.S. border.

Canada is divided into ten provinces and three territories. The provinces are self-governing, in much the same way that the states of the United States are self-governing. The territories, with their smaller populations, were established by federal law and are controlled by the federal government.

PROVINCE BY PROVINCE

NEWFOUNDLAND AND LABRADOR Despite the two names, this is one province, the one that lies the farthest east. The larger, mainland part of the province is Labrador, a land of rocks, swamps, and lakes. Its rugged coastline has promontories that rise directly from the sea. People here live physically isolated lives, and often boats are their only means of transportation.

Newfoundland is a mountainous island with a rocky, rugged coast. There are few cities in this part of the province, and life is centered in small fishing

villages. The land is rich in minerals, and the development of the island's natural resources is an important part of the province's economy. Iron ore and recently discovered offshore oil and gas deposits are the greatest sources of the region's wealth. Pulp and paper and food processing are the main manufacturing industries, while tourism is fast becoming another important industry in the area.

The capital of Newfoundland, St. John's, is one of the oldest cities in North America and was England's first overseas colony.

PRINCE EDWARD ISLAND Prince Edward Island, or PEI, is the country's smallest but most densely populated province. The province's rich, red soil supports a large farming community that produces potatoes as its main crop. Fishing, especially for lobsters, is another important industry in PEI. The capital, Charlottetown, is known as the Cradle of Confederation because it was the site of the historic meeting in 1864 that eventually led to the unification of Canada in 1867.

Houses hug the rocky cliffs surrounding the harbor in St. John's, Newfoundland.

NOVA SCOTIA Like its neighboring provinces, Nova Scotia has a rugged coastline punctuated by numerous bays and inlets—ideal sites for fishing villages.

Mining forms a major part of the Nova Scotian economy, along with tourism and manufacturing. Raising livestock and fruit farming are also important economic activities. Forests occupy about 71 percent of Nova Scotia. The provincial government owns only about one quarter of this woodland, and most of it is used for public parks and reserves. Because of the abundance of forest reserves, hunting—especially for deer and moose—is a favorite outdoor sport for tourists and Nova Scotians alike.

Halifax, the provincial capital and one of the country's main ports, has one of the world's best natural harbors and is the Atlantic headquarters of Canada's navy.

NEW BRUNSWICK Nearly rectangular in shape and with an extensive coastline, New Brunswick is an undulating, heavily forested land. New

Moose roam throughout most regions in Canada.

Brunswick shares the Bay of Fundy with Nova Scotia.

The Saint John River Valley is a fertile oasis that supports farming in New Brunswick. Potatoes, vegetables, cattle, poultry, and pork are the province's major agricultural products. Forest products and food processing are the main manufacturing industries. Zinc, potash, and lead are important minerals. The main catches of the province's fisheries are lobster and crab.

Fredericton is the capital of New Brunswick, and Saint John is its main port and industrial center.

Potatoes grow in New Brunswick. In the background is the 8-mile-long Confederation Bridge, which links New Brunswick with Prince Edward Island.

QUEBEC This is Canada's largest province. Geographically, it is made up of three regions—the plateau-like highlands of the Canadian Shield in the north; the Appalachian Mountain region, which extends partly through the area south of the Saint Lawrence River; and the Saint Lawrence lowlands.

Quebec is a major producer of gold, iron ore, and copper. The Saint Lawrence lowlands are a fertile area where agriculture was once the mainstay of life. While agriculture is still important, it has been overtaken by high technology and manufacturing, especially textiles and clothing.

Quebec has a predominantly French-speaking population that boasts a culture all its own, setting it apart from the rest of Canada. The capital of Quebec is Quebec City, a city with an Old World European atmosphere. Montreal, Quebec's largest city, is a great industrial, commercial, and financial center.

ONTARIO Ontario includes portions of the Canadian Shield in the north and the Great Lakes-Saint Lawrence lowlands in the south. While Ontario's northern terrain is rugged and rocky, its lowlands support a dense and highly industrialized population that produces about 40 percent of Canada's gross domestic product.

The Toronto skyline is dominated by the CN Tower, a telecommunications building and the tallest free-standing structure in the Western Hemisphere.

The cluster of cities around the western end of Lake Ontario is known as Canada's golden horseshoe. It includes Oshawa, the center of Canada's automobile industry; Hamilton, the center of Canada's iron and steel manufacturing; and Toronto.

Ontario is Canada's wealthiest province, and about a third of Canada's population lives there. Ontario is also the most ethnically diverse, with French and English mixing with many other Europeans, Asians, and Central Americans. Cosmopolitan Toronto, Ontario's capital, is Canada's largest city, and its financial and business center. Ottawa, near Ontario's southeastern border with Quebec, is the capital of Canada.

MANITOBA Northeastern Manitoba is part of the Canadian Shield, characterized by hills and forests; the southwestern part is flat. The economy of Manitoba has been built on agriculture, mainly the growing of wheat and other grain crops. Winnipeg, the capital, is the industrial center of the province. It was the first stop in the great rush for land by European settlers who followed the railroad west, and is today home to their descendants—Ukrainian, Hungarian, Polish, Italian, and Portuguese Canadians.

SASKATCHEWAN Two-thirds of this great grain-producing province is flat, prairie lowland, where most of Canada's wheat crop is grown. In addition to grain, Saskatchewan's economy relies on cattle and hog farming, and softwood lumber harvesting. The province is also rich in mineral resources, especially potash (Saskatchewan is a major world producer of potash), oil, and metals, notably uranium.

Regina, the province's capital, and the city of Saskatoon are distribution centers of mainly agricultural products for the surrounding rural areas.

ALBERTA The westernmost of the prairie provinces, Alberta's southeastern region is a dry, treeless prairie. From the prairie, the land rises gradually until it meets the Rocky Mountains in the west. Alberta produces the largest amount of the nation's crude oil and natural gas, and it also produces large quantities of coal. Agriculture is also important, especially grain and

A cowboy drives a herd of cattle on a prairie in Saskatchewan.

livestock. Edmonton is Alberta's capital and its largest city. Calgary is its second-largest city.

BRITISH COLUMBIA British Columbia, or BC, consists almost entirely of the Cordillera, a region of parallel mountain ranges that run in a north-south direction. In the eastern Rocky Mountains, which extend south into the United States, there is a continuous range of wall-like ridges carved by glaciation. The central area of the province consists of several mountain ranges, plateaus, and lake basins. In the west are the Coast Mountains.

The Inside Passage and the Strait of Georgia, which separate the Queen Charlotte Islands and Vancouver Island from the mainland, together form a major navigation channel on the west coast of North America.

Vancouver is BC's largest city, a rapidly growing cosmopolitan center for immigrants from all over the world. Victoria, BC's capital and its second-largest city, is on the southern tip of Vancouver Island.

THE YUKON, NORTHWEST TERRITORIES, AND NUNAVUT The *Yukon*—which means "great river" in Athapaskan—is full of jagged mountains, boundless waterways, and sharp seasonal contrasts. The equally magnificent Northwest Territories, or NWT, occupy roughly 12 percent of Canada. Nunavut, a new territory, occupies 24 percent of the nation. Much of Nunavut is frozen arctic terrain.

Canada's highest mountain, Mount Logan, at 19,550 feet (5,959 m), is in the Yukon, while Canada's longest river, the Mackenzie, at 2,635 miles (4,241

A NEW NAME FOR AN OLD TERRITORY

In 1999, the map of Canada changed. The territory of Nunavut was created as part of a treaty settlement between the native Inuit people and the Canadian government. The region, which includes two-thirds of the former Northwest Territories, is a vast expanse of 808,200 square miles (2.093 million km²), including the waters, in Canada's far north—an area slightly larger than Mexico. It makes up about one-fifth of Canada, covering much of the northernmost section of the Canadian mainland and the many islands that make up the Canadian Arctic Archipelago.

The land is populated mostly by the indigenous Inuit people. They are hardy folks whose ancestors learned how to live in this harsh, frozen land more than 1,000 years ago. However, only about 32,000 people live in this vast space, making Nunavut one of the most sparsely populated places on Earth. Also, since there are few roads—and in most places, no roads—connecting Nunavut to the rest of Canada, it is also one of the most remote.

Nunavut means "our land" in Inuktitut, the Inuit language, and in their own land, the Inuit people govern themselves. The capital of Nunavut, formerly called Frobisher's Bay, and now called Iqaluit, is located on Baffin Island, the largest island in Canada and the fifth-largest island in the world.

km), is in the NWT. The capital cities are Whitehorse (the Yukon), Yellowknife (the NWT), and Iqualuit (Nunavut). The whole region is north of latitude 60°, and part of it is within the Arctic Circle. The Alaska Highway, which runs for 1,488 miles (2,395 km) from Dawson Creek in BC to Fairbanks in Alaska, provides the best road access to the Yukon.

SAINT LAWRENCE SEAWAY The Saint Lawrence Seaway is a system of locks, canals, and channels that link the Great Lakes with the Atlantic Ocean. A monumental feat of engineering, the waterway extends 2,342 miles (3,769 km) from the Atlantic Ocean to the northern tip of Lake Superior. The waterway provides access to ocean-going ships from Montreal to Duluth, Minnesota, on Lake Superior.

The Montreal-Lake Ontario section, which is often thought of as the whole seaway, has four locks that together lift a ship traveling westward about 213 feet (65 m). Between Lake Ontario and Lake Erie, the Welland Canal circumvents Niagara Falls.

The cost of constructing the Saint Lawrence Seaway was shared by Canada and the United States. The two nations have co-managed the seaway since it opened in 1959. The seaway is vital to the Canadian economy, opening the interior of the continent to ocean-going ships and allowing direct, energy-efficient transportation of materials such as iron ore, grain, and coal.

The Welland Canal in Ontario connects two of the Great Lakes: Lake Ontario and Lake Erie.

Three types of bears can be found in Canada. The most familiar is the black bear, which can be found almost anywhere in the country except in the extreme north.

Black bears, which are sometimes brown in color, are good climbers. They are omnivores and will eat almost anything they can find. Vegetation forms a large part of their diet, especially berries and nuts in summer. Bears may become accustomed to scavenging for food in garbage dumps. This brings them into close contact with people. Black bears are normally shy animals, but those that have developed the habit of feeding on garbage sometimes become a nuisance and a danger to people.

The grizzly bear is found in western Alberta, British Columbia, the Yukon, the Northwest Territories, and Nunavut. It is much larger than the black bear and has a characteristic hump over the shoulders formed by the muscles of its forelegs. It gets its name from the light or grizzled fur on its head and shoulders. The grizzly is also omnivorous, often digging for roots, but it will prey on elk, moose, deer, and caribou as well.

Polar bears inhabit the arctic sea coast. They vary in color from almost pure white in winter to a yellow or golden color in summer and the fall. Their thick winter coats and a thick layer of fat under the skin protect them from the cold. They are more carnivorous than the grizzly or black bear, preying mostly on seals.

A WIDE RANGE OF CLIMATE

The climate in Canada varies considerably from region to region, from an arctic extreme where temperatures are below freezing most of the year, to the southern regions where the milder weather of spring, summer, and fall linger for at least eight months of the year.

Atlantic Canada has a fairly changeable climate. There is often a lot of snow in winter, and fog is common in spring and summer. Central Canada, from the Great Lakes to the Rocky Mountains, has a continental climate, with cold winters and hot summers and light, unreliable rainfall. Southern Ontario and Quebec, where the Great Lakes-Saint Lawrence lowlands are located, have cold winters with heavy snowfall and hot but fairly wet summers.

Towering Douglas firs reach to the sky in Cathedral Grove National Park in Nanaimo, British Columbia.

The climate is the most temperate on the western coast, where warm winds blowing from the Pacific Ocean keep winters mild, though cloudy and wet. In the north, areas within the Arctic Circle experience extremely long, cold winters and only a few months with above-freezing temperatures.

FORESTS AND GRASSLANDS

Urbanization has greatly reduced Canada's extensive forest cover. Yet, around 45 percent of the country remains forested—from the northern frontiers to the outskirts of the largest cities. Most of Canada's forests lie within the northern regions, stretching from Newfoundland to the Yukon and extending into western Canada on the slopes of the Rockies and parallel mountain ranges. These forests consist mainly of evergreens and conifers such as fir, spruce, and pine.

Temperate forests of broad-leaved deciduous trees, such as oak, maple, elm, beech, and ash, which shed their leaves in the fall, are found in the milder, southern parts of the country. On the western coast, the mild and wet climate supports the growth of dense forests of tall trees such as the Douglas fir, Sitka spruce, and western red cedar. The Douglas fir is Canada's tallest tree species, growing to on average more than 200 feet (60 m).

In July, fireweed blooms in the Yukon Territory.

In the interior, with light rainfall and a high evaporation rate, grasses range in height from 6 inches (15 cm) to 8 feet (2.5 m). The grasslands of Canada's interior cover most of the prairie provinces and the drier areas of the interior of British Columbia. The grasses have adapted to the dry climate. Their abundant roots readily absorb moisture, which is then conserved in their narrow leaves, and their slender, flexible stalks bend with the wind.

In the coldest parts of the country, the arctic and alpine regions, there are tundra meadows of coarse grasses, mosses, and lichens. Few trees grow here because of the severe climate.

A WILD LAND FULL OF LIFE

The wildlife of Canada is extremely diverse and varies dramatically from region to region, from the pygmy shrew, Canada's smallest mammal, growing to around 3 inches (75 mm) in length and weighing less than an ounce, to the blue whale, the largest known creature, growing up to 100 feet (30 m) in length and weighing 150 tons.

Animals in Canada have adapted to the cold winters. Some migrate south in the fall, some grow a thick winter coat of fur or feathers, and

NIAGARA FALLS

On the international border between Canada and the United States, where the Niagara River separates Ontario from New York state, is the most powerful waterfall in North America. Niagara Falls is a famous destination for tourists on both sides of the border, attracting millions each year. The falls are actually three waterfalls—the Horseshoe Falls, the American Falls, and the Bridal Veil Falls. Combined, they form the highest flow rate of any waterfall in the world. The border goes through them, with most of the Horseshoe Falls being on the Canadian side. The other two falls are on the American side. The Horseshoe Falls are the largest of the three, with a vertical drop of some 173 feet.

Maid of the Mist boats ferry tourists out to the base of the falls, a journey that requires passengers to don ponchos to protect them from the drenching mists. On both sides of the river, the cities of Niagara Falls, Ontario, and Niagara Falls, N.Y. cater to the tourist industry. The Rainbow Bridge connects the two cities.

In 1901, an American named Annie Edson Taylor, 63, went over the falls in a barrel as a publicity stunt and survived unhurt. Since then, other daredevils have tried, and some have died, in similar attempts, which are of course illegal but nevertheless continue.

others hibernate, living off a thick layer of fat accumulated during the warmer seasons.

The inland waters and the seas in Canada support teeming colonies of microscopic plankton and the large number of fish, amphibians, and marine mammals that feed on plankton.

The grasslands support herbivores, such as deer and elk, while the forests provide food and shelter for rabbits, squirrels, and rodents. Birds of prey such as hawks and eagles stay in Canada throughout the year, while other birds, such as insect eaters, fly south in the winter.

Human colonization has caused the extinction of many species of animals in Canada. Some, such as the Dawson caribou, the sea mink, and a penguin-like bird called the great auk, have been hunted to extinction. Others, such as the greater chicken, have declined in number because of the destruction of their natural habitat.

Strict hunting regulations and conservation efforts are turning the tide. Animal species such as the musk oxen, whooping crane, and bald eagle are protected by law. There were once fewer than 1,000 musk oxen and American bison in Canada, but the protection of the law has brought them back from the verge of extinction.

A musk ox grazes in a prairie. These animals inhabit the arctic islands and tundra regions of the Northwest Territories and Nunavut.

INTERNET LINKS

www.canadiangeographic.ca
Canadian Geographic Magazine offers a broad array of features on wildlife, travel, environment, and more.

www.thecanadianencyclopedia.com/en/article/natural-regions
The Canadian Encyclopedia's section on Natural Regions covers Canada's twenty geographical ecozones.

www.nunavuttourism.com
Nunavut Tourism site has information about the people, wildlife, history, and arts of Nunavut.

www.gan.ca/animals/bears+of+canada.en.html
The Global Action network has information about the three kinds of bears in Canada.

HISTORY

Native people occasionally wear traditional dress for festivals celebrating their heritage.

2

THE HISTORY OF CANADA RUNS parallel to the history of the United States in many ways. Like the United States and Mexico, its neighbors to the south, with which it shares the North American continent, Canada was populated by many groups, or tribes, of native peoples for many thousands of years before being "discovered" by European adventurers.

Those explorers came from cultures that were technologically more advanced, and claimed the "new" land for their nations back in Europe. Before long, hordes of Europeans crossed the Atlantic and settled there, pushing out the aboriginal peoples. Like the United States, Canada is a nation of immigrants.

But then Canada's history takes a strikingly different turn. Unlike the United States, Canada did not revolt against England and claim independence. It did not suffer a devastating civil war. Instead, it has had its own challenges to overcome. Canadians have over time struggled with nature and with differences among themselves to create a unique nation. Nevertheless, some tensions remain unresolved even today.

Formerly referred to as Indians, the indigenous peoples of Canada prefer the names *First Peoples* and *First Nations*. Unlike in the United States, where the term *Native American* is common, the indigenous peoples of Canada are usually referred to informally as natives.

EARLY SETTLERS

Most anthropologists agree that Canada's first inhabitants crossed the Bering Strait from Asia more than 25,000 years ago during the Ice Age. They came over a land bridge that then joined Asia and North America. These first immigrants were nomads who traveled the land hunting animals for food. As the weather warmed and the ice melted, animals and people moved south into the heart of North America. Eventually, people learned to gather wild plants and cultivate the rich soil. They stopped wandering and became the first settlers of the land.

Canada's early peoples evolved into many different cultural and linguistic groups. The groups varied as widely as the terrain and gave themselves names such as *Dené*, *Nahani*, and *Kutchin*, which simply mean "the people." European explorers who came looking for a western route to India called them Indians.

Despite their cultural and linguistic diversity, Canada's first settlers shared a deep, spiritual relationship with the land and with nature. But when the Europeans arrived, they brought conflict that caused devastation among the indigenous peoples. The Europeans carried diseases that the natives had no immunity to, such as smallpox. The diseases swept through the vulnerable native populations like wildfire, killing masses of people in a short time. For decades, the indigenous population of Canada declined, threatening the existence of the land's unique cultures.

INDIGENOUS GROUPS

Nomads in the interior plains hunted bison for meat and skins. They included the Blackfoot, Blood, Piegan, Gros Ventre, Plains Cree, Sioux, and Assiniboin. Families lived in groups in *tepees*, which are conical tents covered with skins. The portable tepees were easy to erect and dismantle yet warm and stable enough to withstand winds.

Groups on the western coast, such as the Haida, Tsimshian, Nootka, Coast Salish, Kwakiutl (kwa-ki-yud-l), and Bella Coola, established permanent villages and lived from the bounty of the sea, fishing for salmon and hunting

whales. They built large houses from cedar and carved tall totem poles and other objects from cedar and stone.

The nomadic woodland people in the east—the Algonkians, Mi'kmaq, Montagnais, Naskapi, Ojibway, and Cree—lived in lodges and wigwams constructed of poles, bark, and skins. They were hunters and trappers who followed migratory animals.

The Iroquoian hunters of southern Ontario—the Huron, Tobacco Nation, Neutrals, Mohawk, Oneida, Onondaga, Cayuga, Seneca, and Tuscarora—were superb farmers. They grew corn, beans, and squash and lived in permanent villages of longhouses.

The peoples of the interior plateau were the Interior Salish, Kutenai, Chilcotin, Carrier, and Tagish who hunted and fished for food. Their dwellings ranged from subterranean pits to bison-hide tepees.

The indigenous people of the far north were—and still are—the *Inuit*, meaning "the people." They hunted caribou, whales, and seals. They lived in snow houses called igloos that protected them from the cold. Inside the igloo, a small oil lamp, and body heat, kept people comfortably warm.

Pliable birch bark covers the exterior walls of a Mi'kmaq teepee.

Why did Leif Erikson's landing in North America go unheralded for centuries, leaving Columbus to be given the dubious credit for "discovering America" five hundred years later? Archaeologists have proven that Vikings established a settlement on the northern tip of Newfoundland in today's village of L'Anse aux Meadows. There they identified the foundations of several Norse longhouses, identical to those built in eleventh-century Iceland and Greenland. The archaeologists also found Viking artifacts—some of which indicated weaving and iron-working, activities which were not practiced by Native Americans until after 1500 CE.

Most detailed information about the Vikings' visits to Vinland comes from two Norse sagas, the Saga of the Greenlanders *and the* Saga of Erik the Red. *These two sagas were passed on as oral histories for centuries before being written down. The problem is that the two sagas differ from one another in certain details, so they cannot be treated as historical documents as such. However, they do assert that the Norse men, setting out from Greenland, made several sojourns to the coast of today's Canada.*

Leif Erikson named the places he and his men found there according to their attributes: an icy, barren place he called Helluland ("Flat-Stone Land"); a flat, wooded spot, somewhat farther south, he named Markland ("Wood Land"). But it was the warmer, wooded area that he named Vinland ("Wineland" or possibly "Meadowland") that created the most interest. This land produced fine "wine berries," he claimed. (Some interpretations say "wine grapes" but grapes don't grow in Newfoundland. The

A recreated longhouse at L'Anse aux Meadows.

Norse made wine from many sorts of berries, and it's likely he meant blueberries, or the similar bilberry, which is sometimes called a winberry.)

According to the sagas, Leif's brother Thorvald led an expedition to Vinland in 1003 and spent two years there. Within another year or two, another Viking explorer, Thorfinn Karlsesfni set up a colony somewhere in Vinland. Archaeologists don't know if either of these settlements corresponds to the remains found at L'Anse aux Meadows.

In any event, both the sagas and the archaeological remains agree that the Norsemen did not stay long in "Vinland," and seemingly never returned. Word of the Vinland made it into some of the literature of northern Europe by 1075, and was known to the king of Denmark in that same century. But the news apparently traveled no further.

The short answer to why Leif Erikson was not credited with discovering a new continent is that nothing much came of his findings. They didn't change history and were eventually forgotten or came to be considered mere mythology. However, Columbus' landing centuries later on the island of Hispaniola had an immeasurable impact on the course of history.

FIRST CONTACT

Archaeological evidence shows that in 1000 CE a Viking adventurer, Leif Erikson, established a colony on the island of Newfoundland. It lasted only a few years. For centuries after the Vikings, there was very little European exploration of the new continent, until the search for a new sea route to the East led to the European discovery of the Americas by Christopher Columbus in 1492.

When news of the vastness and riches of the new land reached Europe, it attracted many adventurers such as John Cabot. He briefly explored the waters around Newfoundland and Labrador in 1497 and returned to England with news of rich fishing grounds.

The indigenous people remained relatively unaffected until the first colonizers, the French adventurers and explorers, arrived. One of them was Giovanni di Verrazano, who, in the employment of the King of France, landed in Newfoundland in 1524 and claimed it for France.

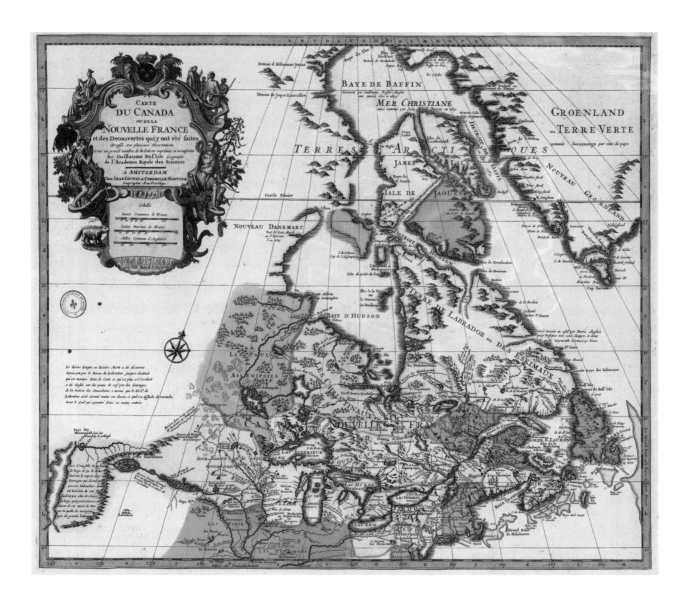

A map from 1730 shows Canada and New France.

EMPIRE BUILDER

In 1534 French explorer and navigator Jacques Cartier sailed into the Gulf of Saint Lawrence and landed on the Gaspé Peninsula. Planting a great cross, he claimed the land for France and for God. In 1535 Cartier made his second voyage up the Saint Lawrence River to the site of present-day Montreal. He became the first European to enter the Canadian interior. On his third voyage to the new land, in 1541, Cartier established a settlement, but this colony lasted only until 1543. Cartier and many other French explorers helped build a vast empire in North America called New France.

FRENCH-ENGLISH RIVALRY

In the early stages of the struggle for control of the new continent, the French outdid the English. French soldiers, missionaries, and explorers such as Jacques Cartier and Samuel de Champlain opened up North America. Adventurous fur traders called *coureurs de bois* (koo-rer de BWAH), or "woodsmen," also played an important role. The coureurs de bois were bold, boisterous adventurers who trapped animals while living a precarious existence in the wild. Many had come from France to escape a life of drudgery. Some had exchanged prison sentences for emigration papers.

The French were lured by the belief that the land they had discovered was rich in gold. They were also driven by the idea of bringing salvation and civilization to the "savages" of the land, and they hoped to gain new land and glory for their king. But instead of gold, they found something nearly as valuable—a large supply of fur, especially beaver pelts.

By the 1670s, New France, the empire in North America, reached from as far north as the Hudson Bay in the Arctic to the Gulf of Mexico in the south. It was run on a *seigneurial* or "lordship" system, which means that the French settlers were granted land by the French Crown in return for services. The seigneurs then subdivided the land to rent it out to other settlers, called habitants, who farmed the land. No more than 10,000 immigrants came to settle during the entire history of New France. Yet they prospered, growing to a population of 60,000 by 1760.

Pressure on New France came from English settlements to the east and south, because French-controlled lands blocked the westward expansion of the English colonies on the eastern seaboard. In the north, the French faced rivalry from the Hudson's Bay Company for dominance of the fur trade. As a result, New France and the English fought an almost continuous series of battles in the seventeenth and eighteenth centuries in which the indigenous communities allied themselves with one side or the other.

"Now, God be praised, I will die in peace," said the dying James Wolfe to his officers on the Plains of Abraham.

"I am happy that I shall not live to see the surrender of Quebec," were among the last words of the Marquis de Montcalm.

The end of New France came in 1759 with the fall of the city of Quebec in which British sea power played an important role. The British navy, controlling the Atlantic, cut the colony of New France off from the mother country. With troops on board commanded by England's youngest general, 32-year-old James Wolfe, a British fleet sailed down the Saint Lawrence River for Quebec. The battle raged for months, climaxing on the Plains of Abraham, west of the city. Wolfe's men formed their famous "thin red line" across the plains, while French forces advanced under the command of Marquis de Montcalm.

After the battle, the Plains of Abraham were covered with the fallen French. Both commanders were mortally wounded. Wolfe lived just long enough to learn he had won, while Montcalm died a few hours later. In 1763 France ceded its North American territories to Britain through the Treaty of Paris.

INVASION AND IMMIGRATION

The new imperial rulers found themselves masters of a population that was different in language and religion. To prevent an uprising, Governor Sir Guy Carleton concluded that French civil and religious rights had to be upheld. In the Quebec Act of 1774, legal status was given to the Roman Catholic Church, to the seigneurial system of landholding, and to French civil law.

When the colonists in North America revolted against British rule in the mid-1770s, Quebec was expected to join the uprising. But that did not happen because the French, who were staunch Royalists and Catholics, had little love for the Protestant republicans in the south. America gained independence, but Britain still reigned supreme in the north.

The American Revolution had a dramatic side effect. Thousands of Americans who had been faithful to England migrated north. Most of these United Empire Loyalists populated the mainly empty shores of Nova Scotia, creating a new colony called New Brunswick, while others settled along the northern shore of Lake Ontario.

The new British settlers soon changed the way Canada was governed. Being accustomed to representative institutions, the Loyalists chafed under French seigneurial and civil law. To avoid conflict, in 1791 Britain created two

colonies, Upper and Lower Canada. Upper Canada was controlled by Loyalist elements, while Lower Canada, with the city of Quebec as its center, remained essentially French in character.

Meanwhile, antagonism grew between British North America and the United States, culminating in the War of 1812. Failure by the British to withdraw from American territories was one reason for the conflict. Another reason was Britain's war with France. Britain prevented American ships from trading with France and forced sailors aboard these ships into its services. In 1812 an American army marched up the banks of the Richelieu River, only to be pushed back by British forces. It was the only time that Canada and the United States fought each other. After several skirmishes in which neither side won, the war ended with the Treaty of Ghent in 1814. Britain and the

The Treaty of Ghent was signed in the Netherlands on Christmas Eve 1814. The man in brown shaking hands is John Quincy Adams, who was the U.S. Secretary of State at the time.

The green, red, yellow, and blue stripes of The Bay department store are prominent in the shopping centers of many towns and cities in Canada. The department store is the modern format of a more-than-300-year-old company. The Hudson's Bay Company, founded in 1670, is the oldest commercial corporation in North America, and one of the oldest in the world. It played a very important role in the opening up of Canada, especially in the northern and western parts of the country. It was originally a fur trading company that had its base in Hudson's Bay in the north. From there it exploited the interior of the continent.

In 1670 King Charles II of England signed a royal charter granting the "Governor and Company of Adventurers" wide powers, including exclusive trading rights in the vast territory called Rupert's Land, where the rivers flowed into Hudson Bay. The company fought with the French for control of the fur trade until 1713 when France acknowledged England's claim to Hudson Bay in the Treaty of Utrecht. In 1821 the Hudson's Bay Company extended its monopoly to the west when it merged with its former rival, the North West Company.

For almost two centuries, the company not only controlled the fur trade but effectively ruled the land, being responsible for providing law and order and government in the region. When it sold Rupert's Land to Canada in 1870, the company retained much of the land on which it had its trading posts and large areas of the prairies. It became increasingly involved in real estate, at the same time doing much business with settlers through the trading posts it had retained.

United States agreed to demilitarize the Great Lakes and extend the border along the 49th parallel to the Rockies.

After the war, the British government, in an effort to strengthen the colonies, helped immigrants to settle in British North America. Others came of their own accord, fleeing the poverty of the early stages of the Industrial Revolution, the starvation wages in bleak factory towns, and an impoverished life on farms. From 1815 to 1855, a million Europeans arrived at the ports of

Halifax, Saint John, and Quebec. They changed the ethnic composition of the country, making the French-speaking population the minority.

In Lower Canada, the French showed their discontent with several uprisings against British domination. The rebellion of 1837 brought Lord Durham from Britain to investigate the cause of the political unrest. He recommended that the two provinces be joined once again into a united Province of Canada. Durham thought unity was the best way to increase Canada's economic progress, the way unification had in the United States. The Province of Canada was created in 1841.

A NEW NATION IS BORN

The colonies of New Brunswick, Nova Scotia, Prince Edward Island, and Newfoundland and Labrador initially had little to do with the Province of Canada. They attracted their share of settlers from Europe. The colonies were directly controlled by the government in London. The 1840s and 1850s were a period of rapid change. Britain adopted a free-trade policy and granted the provinces self-government in local matters. That caused the colonies to develop closer economic ties with the United States.

In 1864 after the leaders of the three maritime provinces of Nova Scotia, New Brunswick, and Prince Edward Island had decided to discuss the possibility of unification of the three provinces, the Province of Canada took it as an opportunity to present a grander proposal—the union of all five into a large country, Canada. The political situation after the American Civil War in the 1860s had much to do with the birth of the new nation. The increased threat that the American army might turn its attention to the British colonies in the north coupled with Britain's desire to see its colonies take more responsibility for domestic affairs cemented the plan.

In 1866 the provinces of Nova Scotia, New Brunswick, and Canada sent delegates to England to present their proposal to the British parliament. Once an agreement was reached, the parliament passed the British North America Act, which came into effect on July 1, 1867, creating the Dominion of Canada. The provinces of Manitoba, British Columbia, Prince Edward Island, Alberta, Saskatchewan, and Newfoundland and Labrador joined the union later.

The word *Canada* is derived from the Huron-Iroquois word *kanata*, which means village.

The Métis are a people created by the union of French and Scottish trappers with indigenous women. They were originally hunters and trackers who lived a seminomadic way of life hunting bison. But bison dwindled as the railroad opened up the west. Afraid that their rights might be ignored, the Métis, under their charismatic leader Louis Riel, revolted and forced the federal government to grant provincial status to Manitoba. Peace was restored for a while, but in 1885 the Métis rebelled again. This time they were crushed, and Riel was executed. In 2003 an Ontario court ruled that the Métis in the province deserved the same rights as other indigenous communities in Canada, as had been promised but not practiced in Section 35 of the 1982 Constitution Act.

A TWENTIETH-CENTURY WORLD POWER

After confederation, Canada continued to attract large numbers of immigrants who filled the cities and farmed the land. The country's products, such as wheat, paper, timber, and minerals, were supplied to an international market, making the country prosperous in the early decades of the twentieth century.

Despite confederation, domestic politics were dominated for many years by the issue of francophone (French-speaking) rights outside of Quebec. The sensitive issue flared again and divided Canadians deeply during World War I when the federal government decided that it had to boost the country's military ranks with enforced conscription.

French Canadians were violently opposed to the decision, seeing it as a move to reduce their already declining numbers. Canadian unity was strained almost to the breaking point. The war took a heavy toll, as more than 60,000 Canadians died in battle. However, when hostilities ended, industrial development accelerated and the economy again prospered. New resources such as lead and zinc and new products such as automobiles and radios found expanding markets both at home and abroad.

The Great Depression of the 1930s hit Canada hard, causing one financial crisis after another, until the outbreak of World War II in 1939. Canada provided munitions and food supplies to the Allied war effort, and Canadian troops played a major role in defeating enemy forces in Italy and in the Allied landings at Normandy, France. By the time the war ended in 1945, some 42,000 Canadians had been killed in the fighting.

The expansion of the economy due to the war effort helped Canada to join the ranks of global industrialized powers. Postwar immigration doubled Canada's population and provided labor for the new industries that developed all over the country.

Today, Canada has emerged as a major world power and is ranked among the most affluent nations in the world. Politically and economically, Canada and the United States have developed very close relations.

HISTORY OF ABORIGINAL POLICY

A native elder participates in a Powwow in Ottawa.

Unlike in the United States, where the Wild West and its cowboy and Native American battles were very much part of American history, there was little hostility between the indigenous peoples and the European settlers in Canada. From the very beginning, both the British and French were interested in getting local cooperation in their fur trade. Then, as the Europeans became interested in working the land, they sought to take the land from the indigenous peoples, not through war but through a series of treaty agreements.

Through these agreements, the indigenous peoples surrendered their rights to the land in return for special reserve lands that were set aside entirely for their use. Between 1764 and 1862 several treaties were signed, mostly covering the fertile agricultural lands on Lake Ontario's northern shore. After confederation, between 1871 and 1921, another eleven treaties opened up land for new settlers from coast to coast.

Nevertheless, Canada's history of interaction with its indigenous peoples was not all benign. The Indian Act of 1876 gave the government great powers to control indigenous peoples living on reserves, generally by governing all aspects of their lives in the hope that eventually they would become assimilated with the rest of society. Even when it was revised in 1951, the Indian Act was still very restrictive. It discriminated against indigenous

SHOULD QUEBEC BE A SEPARATE NATION?

Over the years, some of the French-speaking people of Quebec have felt that their culture and language was diminished by the dominant English-speaking majority in Canada. Some thought the problem might be best solved by having Quebec secede, or separate, from Canada and become an independent country. This philosophy is embodied by the political party Parti Québécois, which was formed in 1968. The party is committed to a program of sovereignty-association, that is, it espouses political independence from Canada while retaining some links, such as a common currency. Popular support for the Parti Québécois resulted in the party being swept to power in 1976 and again in 1981. Yet, in 1980, when asked in a province-wide referendum whether they would support sovereignty-association negotiations with the rest of Canada, the people of Quebec said no.

During the constitutional crisis of 1992, Canadians as a whole and the people of Quebec themselves rejected a new constitutional accord that had been put together by their political leaders. This raised the specter of separatism once again. However, in a 1995 referendum the people of Quebec voted to remain a part of Canada. The separatist movement in Quebec has since faltered somewhat, but only time will tell if Canada remains intact.

Supporters of Parti Québécois cheer election results in 2012.

women by taking away their Indian status if they did not marry an indigenous man. Through a government residential school system, indigenous children were forcibly taken away from their families in order to push the process of assimilation. From the late 1940s indigenous leaders had spoken out against this policy and expressed their people's desire to regain their rightful position of equality with Canadians of other races. Accordingly, in 1970 the government began helping indigenous groups and associations research the treaties and first peoples rights.

In 1972 the National Indian Brotherhood, now the Assembly of First Nations, asked that the first peoples be given control over their own education, so that their children could learn their culture. The proposal was adopted in 1973 by the Department of Indian Affairs and Northern Development. The Canadian government also announced its willingness to consider first peoples' claims. This need to discuss indigenous rights and titles to land, resources, and self-government continues today.

INTERNET LINKS

www.mnh.si.edu/vikings/voyage/subset/vinland/archeo.html
The Museum of Natural History (Smithsonian Institutes) presents a multimedia feature about the Viking journeys to North America.

www.canadahistory.com
Canadahistory.com offers a detailed history from prehistoric times to the present.

www.cbc.ca/history/index.html
Canada: A People's History is an in-depth companion website to a television series produced by the CBC.

www.historymuseum.ca/home
www.historymuseum.ca/virtual-museum-of-new-france/introduction
The Canadian Museum of History site has many features including the Virtual Museum of New France.

GOVERNMENT

A statue of Queen Victoria stands outside the British Columbia Parliament Buildings in Victoria.

VICTORIA R.I.

1837-1901

CANADA HAS MUCH IN COMMON with its neighbor to the south, the United States. The two countries share centuries of history—both were once British colonies—and certainly today they share a great deal of popular culture. Canada, like the United States, is a democracy. In fact, Canada is, geographically, the largest democracy in the world. (The most populous democracy is India.)

However, Canada's government and political system are patterned after that of the United Kingdom. Canada, unlike the United States, is still politically connected to the mother country; they share the same monarch.

Canada is a member of the Commonwealth of Nations, an organization of fifty-three countries, most of which are former British colonies or otherwise once part of the British Empire. Queen Elizabeth II, or the current British monarch, serves as the Head of the Commonwealth, a primarily symbolic position. The Commonwealth includes Australia, New Zealand, India, the Bahamas, nineteen African nations, and others around the world. The United States is not a member.

When Canada became a nation on July 1, 1867, it also became a democratic federation. The powers of government are shared between a central or federal government and the governments of the various provinces that make up the nation. The Constitution Act of 1867,

3

On June 25, 1993, Kim Campbell became Canada's nineteenth prime minister following the retirement of Prime Minister Brian Mulroney. Crawford was the first, and so far only, woman to hold the position. However, she remained in office only until November 4, 1993, when a new election was called and her party, the Progressive Conservatives, lost to the Liberal Party. Her successor, Jean Chrétien, served as prime minister for ten years.

also called the British North America Act of 1867, established one parliament for Canada consisting of the British monarch, the senate, and the House of Commons.

THE BRITISH CROWN

Queen Elizabeth II of Great Britain is the official head of state, which makes Canada a constitutional monarchy. When the queen's successor assumes the British throne, he will also become Canada's king. The monarch is represented in Canada by a governor-general, who has no political power. The prime minister is the head of government. The queen can protect the parliament and the people against any abuse of powers by the prime minister and the cabinet.

Canada's parliamentary system, based on the British parliament, was set up in 1867. Sir John A. Macdonald was the first prime minister

A bronze statue of Queen Elizabeth II riding a horse stands on Parliament Hill in Ottawa.

and Charles Stanley, the Baron Monck, the first governor-general of the newly formed Dominion of Canada. Originally all the governor-generals came from England. The first Canadian-born person to hold the position was Vincent Massey in 1952.

The governor-general is appointed for five years. He or she has no real political power and is not involved in party politics. The governor-general gives "royal assent" to acts of parliament; signs state documents; appoints the leader of the party in power as prime minister; opens, discontinues, or dissolves the parliament on the advice of the prime minister; and reads the "speech from the throne" at the opening of a new parliament and at every new session of parliament.

One of the most important duties of a governor-general is to ensure that the nation is never leaderless. In the event that the prime minister dies or resigns suddenly, the governor-general will appoint a temporary prime minister to lead the nation until a new leader is chosen.

THE EXECUTIVE BRANCH

The executive branch of Canada's government is comprised of the British monarch, the Canadian prime minister, and the cabinet. The king or queen is the head of state, a largely ceremonial, or symbolic, role.

The prime minister is the leader of the party in power and the head of the federal government. He or she holds the most political power, and oversees the real day-to-day business of running the country. The term of office is not fixed, but rather, the prime minister serves until he or she resigns, is dismissed, or dies. A prime minister's duties include presiding over Cabinet meetings, meeting official foreign delegations to Ottawa, and answering questions in the House of Commons. The prime minister lives at the official residence at 24 Sussex Drive in Ottawa.

Prime Minister Stephen Harper greets the crowd in Ottawa in 2011.

Canada's constitution requires that a new government be formed every five years, if not sooner. The governor-general dissolves the parliament and calls for an election. The leader of the winning political party is usually appointed prime minister, and he or she then appoints other elected Members of Parliament to form the cabinet. If the prime minister's party wins a majority of seats in a new election, then the prime minister generally stays on as head of the government. However, if an opposition party wins the majority, the prime minister will usually resign or be dismissed. There are other procedures in place for the removal of the prime minister should the need arise. The ultimate power lies in the hands of Britain's monarch, a step that has never yet been needed.

In 2006, Stephen Harper became Canada's twenty-second prime minister. His party, the Conservative Party, won election again in 2008, and yet again in 2011. As of 2014, Harper was serving his third term in office.

CHARTER OF RIGHTS AND FREEDOMS

Every Canadian has fundamental rights and freedoms that are guaranteed by the Charter of Rights and Freedoms, as contained in the Constitution Act of 1982.

The charter guarantees all Canadians freedom of religion, thought, belief, opinion, and expression, including freedom of the press, freedom of peaceful assembly, and freedom of association.

It protects a Canadian citizen's mobility rights (to live, work, and move to wherever he or she chooses), legal rights (to life, liberty, and security), and equality rights (so that it is an offense to discriminate on the basis of race, origin, color, religion, gender, age, or disability).

It recognizes English and French as the two official languages of Canada and guarantees minority language educational rights, that is, a person's right, if in an English- or French-speaking minority, to be taught in his or her own language.

It is important, however, to realize that the charter expresses basic principles and that it may be difficult to determine a person's exact rights. It is therefore up to lawyers and judges to interpret charter rights and freedoms in accordance with the law and with specific case circumstances.

THE CABINET

The cabinet is the policy-forming body of the government. Each province is usually represented by at least one cabinet minister. The prime minister chooses the cabinet Ministers, and the Governor General formally appoints them. Most cabinet ministers are assigned to one or more government departments, and they are responsible for formulating the policies of their departments. The prime minister meets regularly with the cabinet ministers to discuss and make decisions about various concerns such as government spending, ideas for bills, and new policies, programs, and services.

All ministers share responsibility for the government's policies. They must all support a cabinet decision—at least publicly—even if they do not agree with it privately. If a minister cannot support a decision, he or she must resign from cabinet.

An important feature of Canada's parliamentary system is inherited from the British tradition—that the government must have the support of the majority of Members in the House of Commons to stay in power. If the government loses a vote on a major measure, or on any motion of non-confidence, it is expected to resign or to ask the governor general to call a general election.

THE OPPOSITION

The political party with the second largest number of Members of Parliament forms the official opposition party, called Her Majesty's Loyal Opposition. The leader of that party becomes the leader of the opposition. The opposition performs a very important role in government. It has the responsibility of checking and criticizing government proposals and policies and suggesting ways to improve the governing of the country.

The opposition must also present sound alternative policies and solutions of its own. Each opposition party in the House of Commons has its own leader and appoints critics from among its members. Each critic oversees a certain topic, such as health or defense. The critics present their party's policies on the subject and comment on government policies.

The House of Commons Chamber features vaulted ceilings and stained glass windows depicting the floral emblems of Canada's provinces and territories.

THE HOUSE OF COMMONS

The House of Commons consists of elected representatives from all over the country. Known as Members of Parliament, the representatives come from various political parties and are elected by the people to speak on their behalf.

Representation in the House of Commons is based on population. The number of seats for each province is adjusted every ten years following changes in population size.

The Members of Parliament meet in the House of Commons to discuss social, economic, and political issues and debate and pass laws. Another

In 1982, because of problems caused by the Indian Act and increasing demands by the first peoples for more power and a better standard of living, a special committee on aboriginal self-government was created.

In 1983 the committee recommended that the government establish with the First Nations people a new relationship in which self-government was an essential element.

Accordingly, the Canadian government has committed itself to seeing that the principle of self-government is entrenched in the constitution. Discussions are held regularly on exactly how new laws can facilitate the transfer of a wide range of powers to the various indigenous nations.

The Canadian government states that self government in Aboriginal communities helps the economies of those communities by increasing investor confidence, supporting economic partnerships. These benefits can help improve living conditions.

Among other things, this new relationship led to the creation of the new territory of Nunavut in 1999.

function of the House of Commons is to control the finances of the country through budget and taxation policies.

THE SENATE

The 105-seat senate is the upper house of Canada's Parliament. The senate was formed in 1867 and has two roles. First, the composition of the senate is based on regional representations to ensure that Canada's linguistic minorities, such as Quebec's French speakers, are adequately represented.

Second, the senate reviews laws passed by the House of Commons.

The senate receives proposed laws in the form of a bill from the House of Commons and either passes the bill with or without making amendments to it, so that the bill then becomes law, or rejects it.

Senators are appointed by the governor-general in the queen's name, on the advice of the prime minister. Senators must be at least thirty years old and must retire at age seventy-five.

THE CONSTITUTION

Canada's constitution dates back to the British North America Act (1867). That act brought about the birth of the nation of Canada. But because it was an act of the British parliament, the Canadian government had to go to Britain to amend the act.

In 1982 the British parliament, at the Canadian government's request, passed the Canada Act. That had two significant consequences. First, it included in the constitution the Constitution Act of 1982. Second, it transferred Canada's legislative authority from Great Britain to Canada.

Today, Canada's constitution has four main features. First, it establishes Canada both as a constitutional monarchy and a parliamentary democracy. Second, it makes Canada a confederation with power divided between the federal and provincial levels of government.

The other two features are new. The new act nationalized the constitution and brought it home to Canada, and it established the Canadian Charter of Rights and Freedoms.

CONSTITUTIONAL CRISIS

When a historic agreement was reached in November 1981 between the federal and provincial governments that cleared the way for the proclamation of the Constitution Act of 1982, only the province of Quebec withheld its agreement.

Since the act forms the basis of relations between the federal and provincial governments, the entire *patriation*, or transfer of power from England to Canada, of the constitution depends on an agreement by all

ROYAL CANADIAN MOUNTED POLICE

The Mountie in his scarlet coat is familiar to people around the world as an icon of Canada. The Mountie stands as a symbol of law and order and authority to all Canadians.

When the Canadian government took over control of the vast territories under the Hudson's Bay Company, it realized that something would have to be done to prevent the western and northern wilderness from degenerating into the lawlessness that had accompanied much of the opening of the American West. In 1873 the parliament passed an act that established a temporary police force for the territories. One hundred and fifty recruits were sent that winter to Fort Garry in Manitoba, followed by another 150 later in spring.

The new police force, named the North-West Mounted Police, was organized along the lines of a cavalry regiment, armed with guns and dressed much like soldiers, in scarlet

tunics and blue trousers, to stress their symbolic link with the British army. The new force set up a network of police posts and patrolled the land, effectively curbing the lawlessness of adventurers, many of whom had come from the United States. When gold was discovered in the Klondike, the North-West Mounted Police were immediately sent into the Yukon. Their presence ensured that the Klondike gold rush became the most orderly gold rush in history.

By the early twentieth century, Canadians had begun to realize that the mounted police were here to stay. The Canadian government decided in 1919 to expand the Royal North-West Mounted Police, as it was then known, into a national police force.

When the legislation took effect

in 1920, the mounted police headquarters were moved from Regina to Ottawa, and they became known as the Royal Canadian Mounted Police and gradually took over policing duties all over the country.

Today, the RCMP functions as an agency of the Ministry of Public Safety Canada. Its duties have expanded to include organized crime, terrorism, illicit drugs, economic crimes, and offenses that threaten the integrity of Canada's national borders.

Officers of the RCMP wear a blue uniform today. The scarlet tunic worn by Mounties as popularized in books and movies is in fact worn only on special occasions. But whether in red or blue, uniformed Mounties are on-duty police officers.

provinces. The federal and provincial governments have been trying for many years to agree on such a formula. In 1987 the ministers met at Meech Lake to produce an accord that had to be ratified within three years. But by 1990 both Manitoba and Newfoundland and Labrador had failed to ratify the accord, and it floundered.

In a 1992 referendum, Canadians rejected a constitutional agreement known as the Charlottetown Accord. Things came to a head in 1995 when Parti Québécois leader Jacques Parizeau called for a referendum to allow

The famous Parliament Buildings in Ottawa,

Quebecers to decide once and for all whether they wanted to remain a part of Canada. The margin was close—49.4 percent for separation, 50.6 percent against.

Further attempts at resolving the crisis have also failed. As a result, Quebec remains the only province that has not signed the constitution under which it effectively operates.

OTTAWA, THE NATIONAL CAPITAL

In the mid-nineteenth century, when Upper and Lower Canada were joined to form the Province of Canada, there was such rivalry between the two provinces that neither Toronto nor Montreal could serve as the capital. Instead, the legislative branch had to meet alternately in both cities.

When looking for the site of the new capital, Queen Victoria selected the provincial town of Ottawa (which was formerly known as Bytown, named after Colonel By who constructed the Rideau Canal that cuts through the city) as a compromise, because Ottawa was located on the border between Upper and Lower Canada. Sir Edmund Head, then the governor-general, remarked: "I believe that the least objectionable place is the city of Ottawa. Every city is jealous of every other city except Ottawa." Ottawa thus became the capital of the Dominion of Canada in 1867.

At that time, there was nothing else in favor of Ottawa as the capital. Essayist Goldwin Smith called the city a "sub-Arctic lumber village, converted by royal mandate into a political cockpit." Today, however, Ottawa is living up to its name as the seat of the Canadian government. It is a modern city with a population of more than 883,400, with 1.2 million living in the metropolitan area. It is located at the confluence of three rivers in a beautiful setting that is enhanced by the National Capital Commission with parks and sidewalks lined with flowers.

INTERNET LINKS

www.canada.ca
The official web site of the Canadian government has information about history, arts, culture, heritage, the environment, and more.

www.parl.gc.ca
The home site of the Canadian Parliament includes a portal to the Senate page.

www.aadnc-aandc.gc.ca
Aboriginal Affairs and Northern Development Canada has information about the government of the First Nations.

www.rcmp-grc.gc.ca
This is the home page of the Royal Canadian Mounted Police with history, fact sheets and FAQs.

ECONOMY

Two-man crosscut lumbering saws were once used to cut trees and logs. Today, forestry products are still an important part of Canada's economy.

4

W ITH VAST NATURAL RESOURCES, a stable government, an educated workforce, and a high level of industrial development, Canada has the eleventh-largest economy in the world. Its resources lie above the ground, below the ground, and in the sea. It is a leading producer of forestry products, has the third-largest known oil reserves in the world and, with the longest coastline of any nation, has one of the world's most robust fishing industries.

Canada's rich natural resources have from the earliest times provided for Canadians' basic needs, such as food, clothing, and shelter. It was Canada's natural wealth that attracted the first European settlers and traders who came and worked the land. Today, natural resources remain the backbone of the increasingly diversified and industrialized Canadian economy.

AGRICULTURE

In earlier times, most Canadians were farmers. Many were subsistence farmers, meaning their efforts went mainly into producing enough food to feed their families. If they had enough, farmers would sell their

In 2012, over 16 million tourists arrived in Canada, adding some $17.4 billion to the economy. In addition, tourism in Canada supports 309,000 jobs.

Canola fields glow in the summer sun.

produce in the domestic market. This picture has changed dramatically. Today, farms are fewer in number, but larger in size. The average age of Canadian farmers is growing older and fewer young people are going into the business of farming. Only around 2 percent of the population is engaged in agricultural activity. Despite this low percentage, the average farm can produce much more than before, thanks to technological advances.

Slightly more than half of what Canada produces is exported. The importance of agriculture to the economy is reflected in the assistance farmers receive from the government. There are programs to regulate and promote agricultural education and research and development. Farmers raise livestock and grow grain, fruit, vegetables, and other crops. Most farms grow grain or oilseed, with canola—the seed from which canola oil is produced—recently overtaking spring wheat as the country's number one crop.

The prairie regions of Manitoba, Saskatchewan, and Alberta, home to almost all of Canada's farmland, produce grain and support a large beef-cattle industry.

Saskatchewan produces much of Canada's wheat, and Alberta is the chief producer of feed-grain and beef cattle. Potatoes are the main crop in Prince Edward Island. Quebec is the world's largest producer of maple syrup.

FORESTRY

Forests cover almost half of Canada, or about 10 percent of the world's total forest area. About 1.6 million square miles (4.18 million square km) of forested land, much of which is publicly owned, consist mainly of coniferous trees. Forests are an integral part of Canada's tradition, culture, and history. The health of the forests affects the economy of every province.

Freshly cut tree trunks are loaded onto a truck bound for a sawmill in Quensel, British Columbia in 2013.

Canada is the second-largest exporter of primary forest products in the world, after the United States. Forestry activities include logging and paper and pulp processing. The wood industry manufactures a wide range of products, from lumber and plywood to furniture and prefabricated building materials. Canada exports most of these products, mainly to the United States.

As the health and sustainability of the forests are vital to Canada's economy, the forest industry tries to strike a balance between satisfying the demand for wood and protecting biodiversity and the people's way of life.

Almost as many trees are destroyed each year by fire, pests, and disease as are harvested commercially. Provincial forestry agencies are responsible for seeing that the loss of trees is reduced. Thus, the thinning, pruning, and clearing of forests are part of provincial forest management. Reforestation is also an important aspect of forest management. Millions of trees are replanted each year as part of forest renewal.

Logging is controversial, because the forest directly affects climate and is home to a large number of animals and plants. Canadian forestry faces opposition from conservationists, environmentalists, and First Nations, who claim that loggers often encroach on sacred grounds.

Opposition to logging affects the timber and retail industries alike. Campaigns that dissuade shoppers from patronizing stores selling old-growth wood products have led to falling sales. However, the flip side is that loggers lose their jobs when logging areas come under government protection.

FISHING

Bordered on three sides by water and containing thousands of rivers and lakes, Canada has historically been one of the world's largest exporters of fish products. In 2013 Canada exported more than $4 million worth of fish and seafood products, with lobster being the most valuable export species. More than half of those exports went to the United States, Japan, and the European Union. Canada's main fish exports are cod, herring, crab, lobster, shrimp, and scallops from the Atlantic coast, and halibut and salmon from the Pacific coast.

Fishing was traditionally the main industry in many parts of Atlantic Canada. It still is in some areas, with the provinces of Newfoundland and Labrador and Nova Scotia accounting for 80 percent of the region's catch. British Columbia's fishery, based mainly on salmon, is the country's largest. The federal government is responsible for the management of ocean fisheries and fisheries in national parks. The provincial governments manage freshwater fisheries within their boundaries.

Red sockeye salmon swim upriver to spawn in the Adams River in British Columbia.

MINING

Canada produces more than sixty different mineral products, making the mining industry a major factor in the country's economy. In 2010, there were more than 220 mines producing metal, non-metals, and coal, and more than 3000 stone quarries and sand and gravel pits. Iron ore is Canada's most-produced metallic mineral.

In volume, Canada is one of the world's largest mineral exporters. It is the leading exporter of potash and uranium and ranks among the top five countries in the export of nickel, asbestos, gypsum, salt, molybelenum, titanium concentrate, aluminum, cadmium, cobalt, copper, gold, lead, silver, and platinum. Mineral and mineral products account for about 22 percent of Canada's domestic exports.

Canada exports about 80 percent of its mineral products to the United States, Japan, and the European Union. With the exception of a few minerals, Canada is able to meet its own domestic mineral needs.

The provincial governments are responsible for the exploration, development, conservation, and production of natural resources within their boundaries. To ensure a supply of metals and minerals, the mining industry continues to explore and map mineral deposits and other geological features, and develop new mining methods and equipment.

The rolling hills of the Cheltenham Badlands in Caledon, Ontario, exhibit the colors of the iron oxide that forms them.

ENERGY RESOURCES

Canada's energy is derived mostly from the burning of crude oil, natural gas, and coal, and from nuclear and river power. A small amount comes from solar and wind power and from biomass, which is plant or animal material such as grass, crops, or animal waste.

Canada is the world's third-largest producer of natural gas and the eighth largest in total oil production. A large portion of the country's energy production is used up domestically. Nevertheless, Canada also manages to export energy. In 2011, the country exported about $66.8 billion of crude oil. More than 99 percent of Canadian oil exports are sent to the United States, and Canada is the United States' largest supplier of oil.

Canada's first oil reservoir that was worth extracting commercially was discovered in 1947 in Leduc, Alberta. By 2000 nearly 7 million oil wells had been drilled in the country. Canada has huge potential oil and gas reserves under the Arctic waters and the Atlantic Ocean off the eastern coast.

THE GOLD RUSH

In 1856 a gold prospector, James Huston, discovered a large amount of gold dust along the Fraser and Thompson rivers, which have their source in the Cariboo Mountains of British Columbia. When news of Fraser gold spread south, about 25,000 miners from the United States, Latin America, and Hawaii rushed north. At the height of the Fraser gold rush, about 10,000 miners were spread out over a 200-mile (320-km) area. Mining the Fraser was difficult. Melting snows engorged the river, and mining could not take place until August when the river was at its summer low. In winter the freezing cold and deep snows made mining dangerous and often impossible.

In 1862 an even bigger gold rush began when hopeful adventurers, following the Fraser north, hit the jackpot at William's Creek, in the Cariboo region. Many made a fortune—and squandered it just as quickly—but the real benefits of the Fraser and Cariboo gold rushes were the blossoming of the town of Victoria into a busy city and the opening up of the interior of British Columbia.

In 1896 gold was discovered in the Klondike by a prospector, George Washington Carmack, and his two companions, Skookum Jim and Tagish Charlie. The Klondike was Canada's greatest gold rush. It lasted a few spectacular years, from 1897 to 1900, during which $40 million in gold was mined in the area.

Conditions were harsh. The frozen ground had to be thawed out with wood fires before it could be excavated and the gold-bearing rock recovered. But that did not stop gold fever from infecting the thousands who flocked to the Klondike. Dawson City grew into a boom town. At the height of the rush, the city had a population of about 30,000 people. In 2011, there were only 1,319 residents.

Dawson City in 1898

Canada also has abundant coal reserves. Mined as early as 1639, coal accounts for more than a tenth of Canada's energy supply needs. The provinces of Saskatchewan and Nova Scotia are almost completely dependent on coal for electricity. Canada exports coal to the Pacific Rim countries, Europe, and South America.

Wood is a popular source of energy in rural parts of Canada. Wood wastes and wood chips are also a source of fuel for heating.

A hydroelectric dam in Bassano, Alberta, makes use of one of Canada's many rivers.

Canada is the world's leading producer of hydroelectricity. There are several major hydroelectricity projects in Newfoundland and Labrador, Ontario, Quebec, Manitoba, and British Columbia.

TRADE

In 1988 Canada and the United States signed a free-trade agreement, which would serve as a mechanism to resolve trade disputes between the two countries in a fair and efficient manner. For individual travelers, the free-trade agreement reduced or eliminated customs duties on all goods of U.S. or Canadian origin purchased for personal use. Duties were lifted on consumer items such as computers, calculators, furniture, and clothing.

In 1992 Canada, the United States, and Mexico signed the North American Free Trade Agreement (NAFTA), creating the world's biggest and wealthiest free-trade market. Mexico is Canada's largest trade partner in Latin America. Under NAFTA, import duties that restrict trade and investment among the three countries were to be gradually eliminated. However, since implementation, the agreement has been controversial and has had both positive and negative effects on the three economies involved.

Canada has also committed itself to improving trade through trade organizations. It was an original member of the Asia-Pacific Economic Cooperation (APEC) group and joined the World Trade Organization (WTO) in 1995. Nevertheless, not all Canadians believe that NAFTA and trade

Protesters march in Vancouver to demonstrate against the APEC Conference.

organizations are beneficial to Canada. Opponents of the free-trade agreement fear that it will lead to job losses, business failures, and a flooding of the Canadian market with cheap-labor products. WTO and APEC meetings held in Canada have been met with protests organized by Canadians who feel that such groups harm local economies and that they aid only the rich and powerful.

THE CANADIAN WORKFORCE

In the late 1800s, almost half of all Canadian workers were farm workers. By 2002 the number of farm workers had dropped to 2 percent of the Canadian workforce, and only another 2 percent were employed in other primary industries.

The Canadian workforce of 19.08 million people is one of the most highly skilled and highly paid in the world. The average family income in 2013 was $76,000. Young Canadians entering the workforce prepare for jobs in fields that were unheard of just a few decades ago: advanced robotics, computer programming, agricultural engineering, and satellite communication.

About 76 percent of the Canadian workforce works in the service sector, with the retail trade sector employing the largest number of people, followed by the health care and social assistance sector. Manufacturing employs about 13 percent.

The flexible hours of part-time work and the lower cost of employee benefits it presents to companies have led to a rise in the number of part-time workers in Canada. More women are also joining the workforce. In 2011 they made up 48 percent of the workforce.

WORKING CONDITIONS

Canadian workers have come a long way since the days of a more farm-oriented economy but not without a struggle. Toward the end of the nineteenth century, the Royal Commission on the Relations of Labor and

Capital in Canada revealed the hardships of the working class. People worked long hours, children also worked, wages were low, and money could be deducted as a fine for perceived misconduct.

Today, Canadian workers are protected by labor laws. The Canadian Labor Code regulates federal jobs and provides a standard by which workers in Canada can measure how they are being treated by their employers. Among other things, the code limits hours on the job to a maximum of eight hours a day or forty hours a week. Generally, no more than eight hours of overtime work a week is allowed, and overtime pay must be at least one and a half times the regular rate. Minimum wages are frequently reviewed and adjusted according to the state of the economy and the effects of inflation. Employers must give employees at least two weeks paid vacation every year.

In addition, a human rights code prohibits job discrimination on the basis of race, religion, national origin, color, gender, sexual orientation, age, or marital status.

INTERNET LINKS

www.canadiangeographic.ca/cgKidsAtlas/market.asp
Canadian Geographic, CGKids, Marketplace explains Canada's economy through slide shows, videos, and games at a level appropriate for school-age students.

www.cic.gc.ca/english/resources/publications/discover/section-12.asp
Canadian government site explains the economy in easy-to-understand terms.

www.indexmundi.com/factbook/compare/united-states.canada/economy
This site provides a side-by-side statistical comparison of the U.S. and Canadian economies

ENVIRONMENT

An orca springs from the water near an iceberg in Newfoundland.

FROM THE FROZEN TUNDRA OF THE far north to the Rocky Mountains and forests of the west, the Great Lakes in the south, the thousands of islands and miles of coastline—Canada's environment is its natural treasure. Keeping its landscapes in pristine condition is not only a matter of Canadians taking pride in their country's beautiful scenery. Canada's social and economic well-being depends on sustaining those ecosystems.

Canada has a wide range of ecosystems and natural-resource industries to match. Many organizations, both governmental and private, are involved in assessing and caring for the country's land, water, air, and living species.

Ecotourism is a growing sector of the Canadian economy. Some of the ecotourism projects have been initiated by the indigenous peoples with aid from the federal government. They have gradually come to see ecotourism as a way of ensuring their communities' economic development as well as of encouraging a greater appreciation for nature among Canadians and visitors.

5

THE TREES

Canada's first national park, the magnificent and renowned Banff, was created in 1885 to preserve the beauty of the Rocky Mountains. Today, there are thirty-nine national parks and more than 3,000 provincial protected areas. The national parks, which cover slightly more than 2 percent of the nation's land, are managed by the federal government. The provincial governments manage their own parks.

A forestry worker records information about a juvenile spruce tree in British Columbia.

While Canada is thirty-third in the world in the percentage of land that lies in protected areas, it is among the top in total protected area. In 2012, about 10 percent of Canada's total land area was protected. British Columbia, Alberta, Yukon, Manitoba, and Ontario have the greatest proportion of territory under some level of protection, with more than 10 percent of their land under protection. Nunavut, the Northwest Territories, Quebec, Nova Scotia, and Saskatchewan have 8—10 percent of their territories under protection. Newfoundland and Labrador, New Brunswick, and Prince Edward Island have less than 5 percent of their territory under protection.

Responsible forestry has developed with the parks system. The history of Canadian forestry has many examples of wasteful logging based on the erroneous belief that the forests were an inexhaustible resource.

It became increasingly obvious in the twentieth century that forests were in fact exhaustible and that more responsible forestry practices were needed. In 1906 Canada's first forestry program was introduced at the University of Toronto. Since then, Canadian foresters have come to be regarded as some of the most knowledgeable in the world. The last twenty years of the twentieth century saw rapid improvements in forestry practices, with the replanting and replenishing of forests and greater care given to selecting where and when to cut down trees.

POLLUTION

As global warming threatens much of Canada's economy, pollution, especially from greenhouse gas emissions, has become a major issue. In the first few years of the twenty-first century, Canada suffered an increase in drought due to global warming, and the consequent loss of billions of dollars in agricultural revenue. Unusually mild winters stimulated the mountain pine beetle infestation in pine forests, while hot and dry summers led to record numbers of forest fires, especially in British Columbia. Global warming has also affected Canada's fish stocks, while pollution-related illnesses have raised health-care costs.

The Biosphere was first built by famed architect Buckminster Fuller for the 1967 World's Fair Expo 67 in Montreal. Today it houses an environmental museum.

Acid rain is another threat to Canada's natural beauty. The burning of coal in power plants, the smelting of nickel and copper, and the use of motor vehicles produce harmful gases, such as nitrous and sulfurous oxides, which combine with water vapor in the atmosphere and fall as acid rain. Acid rain pollutes rivers and lakes and damages plant, animal, and human life.

Canada holds national environmental events, such as Environment Week and Clean Air Day, to promote environmental awareness. Carpool programs give special highway lanes in cities to vehicles with multiple occupants, and more energy-efficient homes have been built. People generally realize their environmental responsibility and try to do their bit to protect the environment. For example, an increasing number of drivers are choosing to commute by bicycle rather than by car.

However, critics charge that Canada isn't doing enough to tackle its environmental problems. For example, the country's low gasoline taxes don't encourage conservation.

TRACKING ENDANGERED SPECIES

There are hundreds of animals and plant species at risk in Canada. The exact number varies according to which group is doing the assessment: from 345 species (Environment Canada) to 645 (Committee on the Status of Endangered Wildlife in Canada, or COSEWIC). In general, species are classified as being extinct, endangered, threatened, or extirpated, which means locally extinct in a region in which it used to live, but still in existence in other places. This can also mean the species is now extinct in Canada, but still in existence in other countries.

Destruction of native habitat, excessive commercial fishing and hunting, and pollution are largely the factors that endanger species in Canada, as elsewhere. Global warming is also beginning to have an effect. In 2002, the government of Canada passed the Species at Risk Act, its first endangered species act, so that environmentalists can better research, designate, and manage the threatened populations.

COSEWIC lists eighteen species of endangered mammals in Canada, including two kinds of caribou, three kinds of badgers, a kangaroo rat, and others. It also includes marine mammals, listing seven kinds of whales, including the Atlantic and Pacific populations of blue whales and right whales, two populations of beluga whales, and killer whales, or orcas.

It also lists endangered birds, including the Northern bobwhite, the whooping crane, and the Eskimo curlew; and reptiles, including the leatherback and loggerhead sea turtles. Also, amphibians, fishes, arthropods, mollusks, and varieties of plants.

COSEWIC assesses the risk of extinction for wildlife species based on an unusual process. It draws on science, but also Aboriginal traditional knowledge and community knowledge. Aboriginal traditional knowledge is the complex understanding that Aboriginal Peoples have accumulated about wildlife species and their environment, incorporating aspects of culture, spirituality and history. In a similar fashion, community knowledge relies on any particular group's observations on a species' condition in nature: ecological relationships, changes in distribution and abundance, as well as threats affecting the species.

SOURCES OF ENERGY

A wind farm produces energy in the Rocky Mountains.

Energy generation is one of the largest contributors to air pollution in Canada. By far most of Canada's greenhouse emissions are given off in the province of Alberta, by its large-scale industrial production of petroleum resources. By 2005, emissions in Alberta had increased 47 percent since 1990. Ontario, with its large manufacturing base, is the second largest emitting province.

Relief is in sight, as natural gas, the cleanest fossil fuel, replaces coal and petroleum and the use of renewable energy sources becomes more efficient. In 2010, as part of its participation in the Copenhagen Accord, Canada committed to lowering its greenhouse gas emissions 17 percent by 2020 from its 2005 levels.

Hydropower is a major renewable source, particularly in British Columbia and Ontario. Hydropower is nearly pollution-free, but its production requires the damming of rivers. Dams disrupt river flow and cause surrounding areas to flood. This displaces local wildlife and can disturb the ecological balance of the area. To minimize the impact of dams, the Canadian government has developed smaller hydropower plants, especially in more remote regions.

Nuclear power is also controversial. As of 2013, about 15 percent of Canada's electricity comes from nuclear power, from nineteen reactors online, most of them in Ontario. Of these, eleven plants are scheduled to be closed down between 2014 and 2020. Canada had plans to expand its nuclear capacity over the next decade by building two more new reactors, but these have been put on hold for the time being.

THE UNITED STATES-CANADA AIR QUALITY AGREEMENT

In 1991, the United States and Canada entered into an agreement to address transboundary air pollution. That's pollution that crosses national boundaries on air currents. Pollutants released at one location can travel long distances, affecting air quality many miles away. Such pollutants, of course, do not stop at a country's borders.

The United States–Canada Air Quality Agreement (AQA) paved the way for the two countries to cooperate on a variety of air quality issues, including acid rain, ozone, and particulate matter. Emissions from power plants, manufacturing, and waste disposal contribute to the air pollutants, which can cause serious health problems.

In 2011, the United States and Canada marked the twenty-year anniversary of the agreement. Canada's Environment Minister Peter Kent announced that the AQA had resulted in a 50 percent reduction in the emissions causing acid rain and a one-third reduction in emissions causing smog. These reductions have contributed to significant improvements in air quality on both sides of the border.

Wind power is the latest trend in renewable energy. With the abundance of wind in many provinces, wind power may become the most viable form of clean energy for Canada. Another promising source is biomass, mostly organic waste from which methane gas is derived. The potential of solar power is hampered by the abundance of clouds in coastal regions and by overcast winter days throughout much of the country for parts of the year.

RECYCLING

Recycling is another way in which Canadians try to take care of their environment. The concept of "reduce, reuse, and recycle" has become increasingly commonplace in the country in recent years.

All Canadian cities, and most of the smaller towns, have recycling centers where used bottles, paper, plastics, metals, and other materials can be deposited. Refundable deposits on packaged drink sales have so effectively encouraged recycling that drink containers are now rarely seen on the ground or in the trash. The recycling of hazardous materials such as transmission fluid and motor oil has also been strongly promoted.

Environmental consciousness costs, but Canadians understand that it is necessary. For example, a homeowner who buys a can of paint pays a small recycling fee in addition to the cost of the paint. The Canadian government is also working with the electronics industry to implement recycling programs for old equipment such as stereos and computers.

CLEAN, FRESH WATER

While Canada contains roughly one-quarter of the world's fresh water supply, only 7 percent of that is renewable (non-ocean draining). This water supply is threatened by acid rain and waste, and vast amounts of water are wasted through pipe leaks and inefficient toilets and shower heads—problems the United States also faces.

Canada and the United States co-manage the Great Lakes and have a mutual interest in water conservation. Canada's municipal governments have developed water-conservation programs to encourage residents to save water. Such programs have been quite successful in educating Canadians on the importance of protecting their water supply.

INTERNET LINKS

www.ec.gc.ca
Environment Canada, a government site, covers a wide range of environmental topics.

www.world-nuclear.org/info/Country-Profiles/Countries-A-F/ Canada--Nuclear-Power
The World Nuclear Association lists information on Canada's nuclear power.

www.canadiangeographic.ca
Canadian Geographic regularly covers environmental and endangered species topics.

CANADIANS

A small citizen shows his love for his country by wearing the colors and the maple leaf symbol of the flag.

6

CANADIANS ARE A LOT LIKE Americans, and they are a lot like the British. Canadians, however, are definitely not Americans, except that they are North Americans. And they are definitely not British, except they are subjects of the British monarchy. Canadians have French language, culture, and heritage, but they are not French. Some Canadians belong to nations that existed long before Canada. They are Squamish, Iroquois, Cree, Mi'kmaq, or they are Inuit or Métis—but they are also Canadians.

Canadians struggle to define what it means to be Canadian. They find the answer in the story of their past, the reality of their present, and a shared vision for their future.

The early story of Canada is one of its people—the original inhabitants of the land, the colonizers from Europe, and the immigrants who came from afar seeking a better future—and the challenges they faced. For the indigenous peoples, the challenge was first to learn to survive off the land. Later it became a struggle to maintain and preserve their ways of life. For the colonizers and immigrants, the challenge was to learn to adapt to the new and often hostile land.

ROOM TO BREATHE

Canada is the world's second-largest country in land area, and one of the richest. Despite a history of immigration, it is one of the most thinly populated countries in the world, ranked 38th by population size. The 34.8 million people living in Canada are not evenly distributed across the ten provinces and three territories.

Much of the north remains largely uninhabited. Around 90 percent of Canadians live within 100 miles (160 km) of the U.S. border, with southern Ontario being the most densely populated area. Large parts of Nova Scotia, New Brunswick, and the Gaspé Peninsula in eastern Quebec are thinly populated.

A NATION OF IMMIGRANTS

Immigration has played an important part in the history of Canada. At the time of Confederation in 1867, the descendants of European immigrants, United Empire Loyalists, and First Peoples made up the population.

The first settlers were the English and the French. In time, they were followed by Scottish, German, and Swiss immigrants who settled in Nova Scotia. During the American Revolution (1775—1783), about 50,000 colonists who were loyal to England left America and settled in the Atlantic provinces and Ontario to avoid being part of the new American republic. The great potato famine in Ireland in the mid-nineteenth century brought tens of thousands of Irish settlers.

IMMIGRATION DISCRIMINATION

Not everyone who came to Canada in the nineteenth century received an open-arms welcome from Canadians, who were then mostly of English heritage. When the government was actively recruiting prospective immigrants, it had a scale of preferences based on the idea that certain ethnic groups would fit best into Canada's established community. British and American settlers were "preferred," followed by French, Belgians, Dutch, Scandinavians, and Germans. Italians, Slavs, and Greeks were less desirable, followed by Asians and Africans.

But preferred or not, people from other countries kept coming in the belief that they could have a better life in Canada. Many of the early immigrants gravitated to the cities rather than remain in the isolated countryside. They provided the labor needed in mines, lumberyards, and factories, and they worked on the railway, cleared land, and helped build settlements.

Many Canadians did not take kindly to their presence, vital though it was. Racist immigration laws were passed and enforced. They included several anti-Chinese laws, which first imposed a "head tax" on every Chinese person entering the country.

It culminated in the Chinese Immigration Act of 1923, which prohibited any more Chinese from entering Canada. That act stood for twenty-four years before it was repealed. Chinese immigrants who were already in Canada were denied citizenship rights and the right to vote.

Now things are very different. Mindful of their checkered past, Canadians have enshrined within their society a broad framework of laws and policies such as the Charter of Rights and Freedoms, the Human Rights Act, and the Multiculturalism Act. These ensure that all individuals, regardless of where they come from, have a right to equal opportunities within Canadian society.

Today, Canada is one of the world's most tolerant and multicultural countries.

The late nineteenth century also saw the first wave of Ukrainian immigrants. They were fleeing from the extreme poverty, overpopulation, and discriminatory policies of their homeland, which was under the Austrian monarchy. Most of them settled in the prairie provinces.

Asians were also an integral part of the early history of immigration in Canada. Poverty was usually the reason why many Chinese, Japanese, Pakistanis, and East Indians left their homelands. Many of the first Japanese who settled in Canada emigrated to escape serving in the Japanese army when military conscription was introduced in Japan in 1873.

At the start of the twentieth century, the Canadian government began a big push to populate the huge, empty prairie lands. Through a massive publicity campaign, Europeans, then beset by poverty, overcrowding, persecution, and other troubles, were lured across the sea by the promise of free land—all they had to do was clear it, farm it, and make it their home. From 1910 to 1914, about 3 million settlers flooded into Canada.

A POPULATION BOOM

Since World War II, Canada has experienced another period of population growth that was first fueled by the post-war "baby boom." Thousands of soldiers returning from battle in Europe and Asia got married and started families at the same time, creating a sharp uptick in the birthrate. Around the same time, tens of thousands of immigrants from eastern and southern Europe were admitted. In addition, Canada took in many Ugandan, Chilean, Czechoslovakian, Hungarian, and Southeast Asian refugees.

By the 1970s, the country had become known as a land of opportunity. People facing an uncertain or troubled future in their home countries continued to look to Canada as a safe haven. In 2002 a new Immigration and Refugee Protection Act was adopted. The state of the country's population, economy, society, and culture are all taken into consideration when determining policy, while the aim is to help families reunite. The act does not discriminate on racial or ethnic grounds, and recognizes Canada's obligation as one of the world's most favored countries for refugees.

FIRST PEOPLES TODAY

Canada had an indigenous population of about 350,000 when the Europeans arrived. In the following decades, this population declined because of disease, starvation, and warfare, threatening the existence of their unique cultures. At the time of Confederation in 1867, there were between 100,000 and 125,000 First Nations people in Canada.

The downward trend has reversed, and today the Aboriginal population is growing at a faster rate than the rest of the population. In 2001 more than one million Canadians reported having aboriginal ancestry. Inuit make up less than 10 percent of the indigenous population.

As a result of treaties, most of Canada's First Nations peoples live in communities called "Indian bands" on reserves set aside for their exclusive use. But the reserves are not as rich in resources as was their ancestors' land.

There are 614 bands living in 3,100 reserves. In the 2011 census, of the 637,660 First Nations people who reported being Registered Indians, nearly one-half lived on an Indian reserve. The bands vary in size, the largest being the Six Nations of the Grand River in Ontario, which has about 24,000 members. Socially and economically, the Aboriginals are generally poorer than other Canadians due to the discrimination they faced in the early years. But their situation is improving. Close to half of all First Nations peoples in reserves depend on social assistance from the government.

Native people participate in an annual Squamish Nation Powwow in Vancouver in 2010.

The unemployment rate among the indigenous population is more than three times that of the national population. But one must remember that the number of unemployed includes many people who continue their traditional forms of work, such as hunting and fishing, which earn them just enough to live on.

With improving conditions, the First Nations peoples are slowly making the government and other Canadians aware that they were once free, self-sustaining peoples. Today, aboriginal councils manage almost all aboriginal affairs. More indigenous children are attending school, some operated by the bands, some by the government. Aboriginal Business Canada, a government agency, has provided financial and other support to around 5,000 aboriginal businesses.

The indigenous peoples are seeking their own forms of self-government. With the creation of Nunavut, they have begun to achieve that goal, which they hope will enable them to assume their proper place in Canadian society while maintaining the rich diversity of their traditional cultures that evolved over thousands of years before European contact.

IS THERE A CANADIAN IDENTITY?

In a large country consisting of immigrants from many lands, it is not easy to pin down the Canadian identity. The problem seems to have provoked an endless discussion among Canadians on the question "Who are we?" But it is a discussion done with typical Canadian humor, self-deprecating and good-natured.

Attitudes are now changing. Canadians have become more comfortable with themselves. Where Canadians were once restrained in showing their emotions, they are now less ambivalent about displaying their pride for their country. Canadians have always been proud of their country, but it is traditionally a quiet form of patriotism that bubbles to the surface only on occasions such as winning the hockey gold at the Winter Olympics.

Canadians see themselves as peaceful people with little interest in wars and conflict and running other peoples' lives. If Canadians should get involved in disputes, they are very likely to consult all parties involved and work on getting a compromise that benefits all. Canadians, in fact, pride themselves as mediators.

Perhaps the reason for the pacifist attitude of Canadians is a history that is remarkably free of bloodshed, war, or revolution, which often mark the birth of a nation. Canada outgrew its dependence on Britain in a slow and hesitant manner. In fact, Canada never completely severed ties with Britain and still has a close relationship with its former colonizer. There is a general view that it took almost a century after Confederation for Canadians to come to recognize themselves as Canadians.

But Canadians' pride for their country extends beyond sports and diplomacy. They love their wide open land and its resources, and they greatly appreciate the freedoms that their constitution has given them: to vote, to practice one's religion, to work or go to school regardless of one's ethnic heritage or gender, to speak one's own language, to voice one's personal opinion.

Canadians accept themselves for who they are—a peace-loving united group of people with diverse backgrounds and ways of seeing the world.

INTERNET LINKS

www.bbc.com/news/world-radio-and-tv-18086952
BBC News: "What Does It Mean to Be Canadian?"
This is an interesting article about the Canadian identity.

www.pch.gc.ca
The Canadian Heritage section of the Government of Canada has a page about Canadian Identity.

www.firstpeoplesofcanada.com
First Peoples of Canada site is rich with information, maps, and images.

www.cbc.ca/news
The news site of the Canadian Broadcasting Corporation (CBC) has national and Aboriginal news.

LIFESTYLE

Adventurous Canadians paddle a canoe on Lake of Two Rivers in Ontario.

7

CANADA IS BASICALLY A GOOD PLACE to live. Of course, that doesn't mean there are no instances of poverty, crime, disease, or other miseries common to civilization, but there are less than in many other places. Individually, many Canadians are trying to live a healthier, more environmentally friendly lifestyle.

FAMILY LIFE

In Canada, as in every country, the family is a most important unit of society. However, just as in other wealthy industrialized nations, the size of the average Canadian family is getting smaller. People are marrying later in life and having fewer children than their parents did. There is also an increasing tendency for young, single members of the family to leave home and set up their lives and careers away from their hometowns. Other factors that have contributed to the shrinking of the Canadian family include an increasing number of single-parent families and of unmarried women choosing to have children and raise them on their own.

Since World War II, more and more couples in Canada have been entering into relationships and forming families without actually getting married. Such family arrangements, known as common-law unions, are found especially among younger or divorced Canadians. Nevertheless, many common-law unions eventually end in marriage. In 2005, Canada

A black bear cub from Canada named Winnipeg (or "Winnie," for short) was donated to the London Zoo in 1915, and quickly became one of the most popular attractions. A little boy named Christopher Robin Milne loved to go to the zoo to see Winnie. The bear inspired the boy's father, A.A. Milne, to write stories about Winnie-the-Pooh.

A couple celebrates their wedding in Toronto.

became the fourth country in the world to legalize same-sex marriage.

Since 1968, when divorce laws were relaxed in Canada, divorce has been on the rise. Since the mid-1980s, almost half of all marriages in the country have ended in divorce. However, that trend may be reversing. From 2006 to 2011, the number of new divorce cases decreased by 8 per cent, dropping steadily each year. One reason for the decline in divorce may be a corresponding decline in marriages. A 2010 study found that for the first time in history, there were more unmarried people than legally married people age fifteen and older in Canada.

GROWING UP IN CANADA

Most children start school by age five or six. By Canadian law, children must attend school from ages six through sixteen. School usually begins with kindergarten and finishes in either eleventh or twelfth grade. Generally, elementary school runs from kindergarten to sixth grade, junior high school covers the years from seventh to eighth or ninth grade, and senior high school starts in ninth or tenth grade and ends in eleventh or twelfth grade.

After graduation, students find a job or continue formal education at community colleges, technical institutes, or universities. The University of Toronto, University of British Columbia, and McGill University in Montreal are three of many internationally acclaimed Canadian universities.

Smoking among young people continues to be a concern. In 2012, about 11 percent of Canadian teens ages eleven to fifteen said they smoked cigarettes. However, that rate rose to 20 percent for young adults ages twenty to twenty-four, and was the highest for people ages twenty-five to thirty-four. Twenty-two percent of that age group were smokers.

SOCIAL SERVICES AND SECURITY

The Canadian government provides many social services to the public. Health and social programs, such as Medicare, Canada Pension Plan, Canada Assistance Plan, and a Guaranteed Income Supplement ensure that Canadians will be cared for in the event they become disabled, unemployed, or otherwise unable to provide for themselves.

Seniors dance outdoors at a festival in Rocky Harbour, Newfoundland.

Depending on which political party comes to power, whether liberal or socialist in outlook, these social programs may either be cut back to reduce the financial burden they place on the government or increased to be compatible with the social philosophy of reducing inequality in society. Low-income families with children under age eighteen receive monthly payments, called child tax benefits, from the government to help with the financial cost of raising their children.

Both employers and employees make contributions to the Canada Pension Plan, which then provides a pension to workers and their families when they retire. Employment Insurance is a nationwide program that helps people who are out of work.

WOMEN IN CANADA

The organized women's movement in Canada developed in the late nineteenth century, focusing mainly on gaining voting rights for women, access for women to higher education, and equality in the work place.

In the late 1970s, women's organizations brought cases of wife and child abuse to the attention of the public. This led to a law that permits intervention in cases of domestic assault. Women were also successful in getting the principle of sexual equality incorporated in the Charter of Rights and Freedoms that formed part of the 1982 Canadian Constitution.

Women make up an increasing proportion of Canada's workforce. More than twice as many women now hold jobs as did in 1976. In 2009, the number of employed women outnumbered men in Canada for the first time. Part of the reason is education—in 2011, Canadian women earned 52.7 percent of university degrees.

Despite the advances that have been made with regard to the status of women in society, they still have a way to go in wage parity. Between 1997 and 2007, the proportion of women matching or exceeding their husbands' earnings climbed from 37 percent to 42 percent.

Nevertheless, in 2007, women still earned an average of 71.4 percent of what men earned. Part of the reason is that women are much more likely to hold part-time jobs; some 70 percent of part-time workers are women. This is because women devote more hours per week than men to activities such as child care and doing the many chores relating to running a household.

Women are aware of their right to independence and to control their own lives. They join unions and other organizations that aim to establish equal pay for equal work, maternity leave and benefits, adequate daycare facilities, the end of discrimination in the workplace, and protection against sexual harassment. However, the working and social conditions of Canadian women are certainly not exclusive to Canada. They are similar to those in most Western industrialized nations.

GETTING FROM ONE PLACE TO ANOTHER

Canada is so large that since its earliest days the method of getting from one place to another has been an important aspect of life. The country owes its unity to the railway, which overcame *muskeg* (bogs), swamps, and mountain ranges to link the Pacific and Atlantic coasts.

Canada has two major railways: the Canadian Pacific Railway and the Canadian National Railway. There are also several smaller local ones. Passenger rail service is provided by a government company called VIA Rail, but people usually drive, use intercity bus services, or travel by air over long

HEALTH CARE

Canada's health care system is one of the country's greatest points of pride. It's designed to ensure that everyone receives medical treatment regardless of their ability to pay. The program is an interconnected system of ten provincial and three territorial health insurance plans, which Canadians call "medicare." It is publicly-funded, meaning it is financed through taxes. Many health services are free and delivered by private health care practitioners. People can choose their own doctors and be assured that their medical information is confidential.

According to the Canada Health Act of 1984, the provinces and territories organize and finance their own health insurance plans. The federal government also contributes. People pay toward the plan, but the amount they pay varies according to their income level. For elective procedures that the system doesn't cover, people can choose to supplement their insurance or pay out of pocket. In general, the government pays for about 70 percent of Canadians' health care costs.

In remote areas where there are no provincial or territorial services available, the federal government provides primary care and emergency services. It is also involved in the regulation of medicines, foods, and medical devices; consumer safety; the monitoring of disease; and disease prevention. The federal government also supports health research.

Canadians overwhelmingly approve of their health care system. In 2008, a study found that 91 percent of Canadians prefer their health care system to that in the United States. Nevertheless, Canadian health care program continues to evolve and change. The system faces challenges from financial constraints, the aging of the population, and the high cost of new technology.

distances. As a result, VIA Rail cut back on its services, though lately this trend has begun to reverse. A mainstay of VIA Rail is its popular Western Transcontinental service from Vancouver across the Rocky Mountains to Edmonton, Winnipeg, and Toronto.

Major international airports link Canada with the rest of the world. There

THE ALASKA HIGHWAY

Canada's first roads were built for military purposes. A prime example is the Alaska Highway, nicknamed the Alcan Highway. The Japanese attack on Pearl Harbor in Hawaii in 1941 made the U.S. government realize the vulnerability of Alaska's shipping lanes to an attack. An inland route to Alaska was thus deemed a military necessity.

In exchange for the right-of-way through Canada, the U.S. government paid for the construction of the highway. For eight months in 1942, 11,000 American soldiers and thousands more Canadian and American civilians worked on the highway from both north and south. In 1946, when the war was over, the Canadian portion of the highway was turned over to the Canadian government.

The Alaska Highway stretches 1,488 miles (2,395 km) from Dawson Creek, British Columbia, to Delta Junction near Fairbanks, Alaska.

are also many large and small airports throughout the country that cater to domestic travel. Canada's main international airline is Air Canada. Other smaller air carriers offer air links with most of the communities across the country. They are especially important to the small, remote communities in the north that get most of their services by air.

Most important is the network of roads that crisscross Canada. Roads of all kinds ensure that people and goods can travel to almost every part of the country. The Trans-Canada Highway, which is 4,725 miles (7,604 km) long and took more than half a century to complete, stretches from St. Johns, Newfoundland and Labrador, to Victoria, British Columbia. Intercity buses provide an even more important link between cities than either air or rail. The three largest bus companies in Canada are Greyhound, Voyageur, and Gray Line. They allow Canadians to travel anywhere from the Pacific to the Atlantic and down into the United States. In 2005 there were about 18 million passenger cars in Canada. Cars are necessary for work, shopping, and recreation. Many families own more than one vehicle.

Even when they are not on the move, Canadians cover the miles by way of electronic communication, much of it wireless. People stay connected by way of smartphones, laptops, and tablets. In fact, Canadians send more than 270 million text messages per day! Canada's wireless carriers now offer coverage to more than 99 percent of the nation's people.

As of 2011, about 81.6 percent of Canadians had access to the Internet, and 77 percent of those online engaged in e-commerce. Those numbers are rapidly rising. Indeed, there are so many electronic devices in use in Canada—just as in other highly industrialized countries—that they are causing a new kind of environmental waste problem, the problem of how to safely dispose of e-waste.

INTERNET LINKS

www.oecdbetterlifeindex.org/countries/canada/
The OECD Better Life Index findings for Canada.

www.heroines.ca
A guide to women in Canadian history.

www.hc-sc.gc.ca
Health Care Canada explains the national health care system.

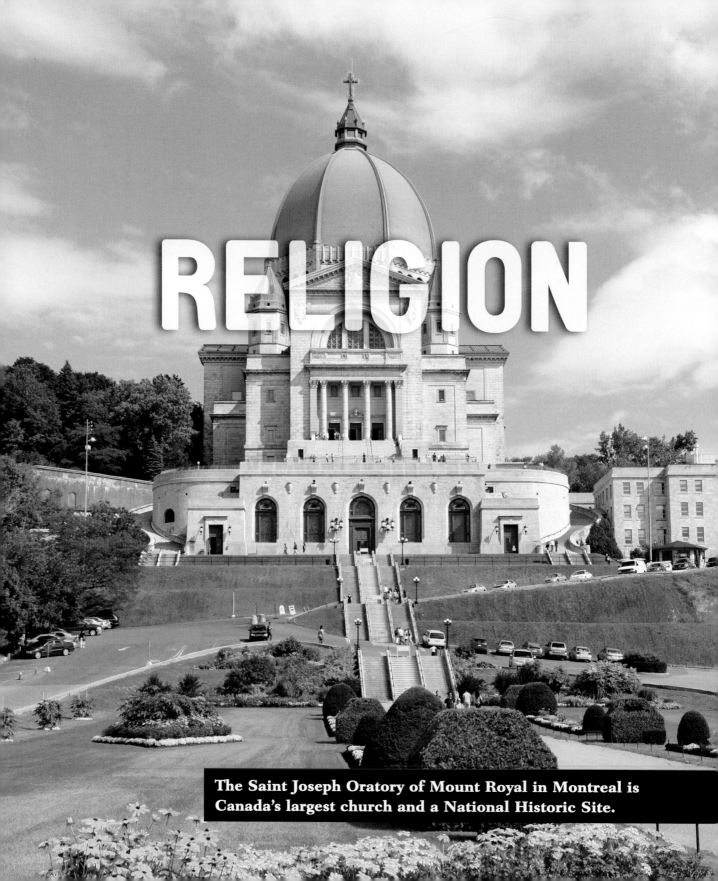

RELIGION

The Saint Joseph Oratory of Mount Royal in Montreal is Canada's largest church and a National Historic Site.

8

CANADA IS A LAND OF MANY religions, but most of all it is a land of freedom. Freedom of religion—and freedom from religion—is a hallmark of Canadian society in the twenty-first century. Canada's past, however, is another story. The nation's history is inextricably bound with religion.

The indigenous peoples were filled with the spirit of the land and a reverence for nature and creation. When the French explorers came, they brought with them missionaries who introduced Christianity to the indigenous peoples. Canada's First People were not accorded the freedom to maintain their ancestral beliefs; over the centuries, European colonizers tried to snuff out the native religions.

However, ironically, for people suffering from religious persecution in their homelands overseas, Canada became a refuge. They went to Canada, where they could practice their own faiths in peace. The millions who followed in the footsteps of the early immigrants to Canada introduced even more diversity into the religious fabric of the country.

Today, the spiritual ways of Canada's indigenous people are finally respected. The freedom to practice one's own religion is enshrined in and protected by the Charter of Rights and Freedoms.

"The white men have offered us two forms of religion: the Roman Catholic and the Protestant. But we in our Indian bands have our own religion. Why is that not accepted too? It is the worship of one God, and it was the strength of our people for centuries."
– Saskatchewan Cree Chief Thunderchild, late nineteenth century

This cross commemorating Jacques Cartier is on l'île St. Quentin (St. Quentin Island) in Trois Riviers, Quebec.

THE SPIRIT OF THE LAND

The first peoples of Canada consist of many communities, but all of them have in common a deep spiritual relationship with the land and nature. They see themselves as a part of a world of interrelated spiritual forms.

When people hunted animals for food, they treated the animal with great respect. A hunter might talk or sing to a bear before killing it, assuring the animal that its death was necessary only because he and his family needed it for food. A tree would not be cut down to build a canoe until its spirit was first appeased.

Myths were very important to the indigenous peoples. They told the story of creation and the origin of the moon, the sun, and the stars. They explained the meaning of various religious rituals. Visions and dreams had a lot of significance. Young people might seek a vision of their guardian spirit, who would reveal to them their personal chants, which they were to sing when in danger.

CONVERTING THE FIRST PEOPLES

When the French and the English reached the shores of North America, they perceived the indigenous peoples as savages and heathens and believed that it was their task to bring enlightenment to them. Jacques Cartier introduced Christianity to Canada in 1534 when he landed on the Gaspé Peninsula and planted a great cross. Samuel de Champlain followed, bringing with him four gray-robed Recollect friars of the Franciscan order. They were the first missionaries from France and were quickly followed by Jesuits, Sulpicians, Ursulines, and others.

HEALING RITUALS OF THE FIRST PEOPLE

Intricately woven into the nature-based belief systems of the indigenous people were healing rituals. Knowledge of healing herbs and other natural medicines was passed along from generation to generation over the centuries. The shaman, or medicine man, was a powerful member of a community who had ancient knowledge of healing practices

The Ojibway underwent a purification ritual, entering a sweat lodge where the scented vapors of an intensely hot, herbal sauna cleansed their bodies and spirits.

The Huron and Iroquois peoples had curing societies. The Iroquois False Face Curing Society used carved wooden masks that they believed possessed a spiritual force. Those forces gave special curative powers to those who wore the masks.

Transformation masks, used by the Pacific Coast peoples, were worn during religious ceremonies to show their belief in the inter-connectedness of people and animals. The masks opened and closed to reveal either a human or an animal face as the wearer pulled the strings.

All the nations had their own ways, and Canadian indigenous people still draw on much of this knowledge today. What the healing practices have in common is that they are holistic in approach. The mind, body, and spirit are all seen as parts of the individual, and one part cannot be treated without attention to the whole. Illness is considered a physical manifestation of spiritual, mental, emotional, and physical disease. Traditional healing might include a combination of spiritual ceremonies, music and dance, herbal medicines or animal remedies, and counseling, which might include the input of the tribal elders. The accumulated knowledge of the elders is considered a vital source of healing power.

CLAIMING THEIR OWN

As the European settlers opened up the continent of North America, the church became their constant companion and source of comfort in an undiscovered, hostile land. The English colonies were predominantly Protestant, while New France was Roman Catholic.

The French clergy faced great opposition in their attempts to convert the indigenous peoples, but they had it much easier among their own people. The French missionaries set up schools and hospitals, collected church tithes from the farmers, and had a powerful moral influence in French-Canadian society.

There were Anglican military and naval chaplains in Newfoundland and Nova Scotia before 1750. However, Anglicanism really got a foothold in Canada with the flood of Protestant Loyalist refugees who fled north during the American Revolution.

While adventurers and explorers strove to monopolize the fur trade and the land, the missionaries spread their faith. Not surprisingly, the missionaries were often frustrated in their attempts to convert the indigenous peoples. Many of the missionaries gave their lives for their cause, such as the Jesuit priest Jean de Brébeuf and his fellow missionary, Gabriel Lalemant,

Jean de Brébeuf

who suffered a horrifying death at the hands of the Iroquois in 1649.

In the long run, however, it was the indigenous people who suffered the most.

ROOM FOR ALL BELIEFS

Other missionaries who came after the English and the French brought with them their own churches. The Dutch arrived with their Dutch Reformed Church. The Lutherans came from Sweden and Germany. The Scots

Marie Guyart, born in 1599 in France, was only nineteen years old when her husband died, leaving her with a young son. In 1620, she had a mystical vision which changed her life. She devoted herself to God and in 1631 entered a convent and became an Ursuline nun. In another vision, she was inspired to go to New France to help establish the Catholic faith in the New World.

She sailed to Quebec in 1639 and started a convent and school, the first school in Canada. Marie de l'Incarnation, or Marie of the Incarnation, as she was called, ministered to the French colonists and also to the indigenous children, often in their own languages, which she had learned. She created dictionaries in Algonquin and Iroquois (which had no written language system) and wrote books about Catholicism in those languages. She earned herself the title of "spiritual mother of New France." Today, the Ursuline Monastery of Quebec is one of the National Sites of Canada.

Marie was beatified in 1980 by Pope John Paul II; in 2014, Pope Francis canonized her as a saint. The Anglican Church of Canada also celebrates her life and works with a feast day on April 30.

introduced Presbyterianism when they emigrated to Nova Scotia in the nineteenth century.

Immigrants from Asia brought their own beliefs: Buddhism, Sikhism, Hinduism, and Islam. As of 2011, about eleven percent of Canadians self-identify as Muslim, Sikh, Hindu, Buddhist, Jewish, or an adherent of other religions (including Orthodox Christianity).

'KILL THE INDIAN IN THE CHILD'

The effort to force the aboriginal people to assimilate went further than conversion to Christianity. When Canada became a nation in 1867, the new government wanted the indigenous people to give up the old ways and assimilate into Canadian society. At the time, the thinking was that they would be better off by learning to be modern Canadian people. Native ways were thought to be just so much hocus-pocus at best, and at worst, dangerous, barbarian, and uncivilized. To put an end to it, government threw the full force of its power against the ancestral religions and customs of the Natives.

The Indian Act of 1876 set out a legal framework for establishing government control over every aspect of Native life. The legislation banned important tribal ceremonies, including the Potlatch, the Sun Dance, and other rituals.

Around the same time, the Canadian government created a system of residential schools for indigenous children. (A similar program was underway in the United States.) Young native children were sent to boarding schools far from their communities. There, they were educated in the language, religion, and customs of the white man. The schools were run by various churches. In 1920, under the Indian Act, it became mandatory for every Native child to attend a residential school and illegal for them to attend any other educational institution.

The residential school system endured for most of the twentieth century. It had a devastating effect on indigenous families and on the individuals themselves. In 2008, Canadian Prime Minister Stephen Harper issued an official apology, saying, "Two primary objectives of the residential school system were to remove and isolate children from the influence of their homes, families, traditions and cultures, and to assimilate them into the dominant culture. These objectives were based on the assumption Aboriginal cultures and spiritual beliefs were inferior and unequal. Indeed, some sought, as it was infamously said, "to kill the Indian in the child." Today, we recognize that this policy of assimilation was wrong, has caused great harm, and has no place in our country."

A TREND TOWARD NONAFFILIATION

Today, Canada remains a predominantly Christian nation, but the religious landscape is changing. Partly this is due to the influx of people from parts of the world where other religions are dominant. But it is also because the number of people who do not belong to any religion has grown, particularly among younger Canadians. In 2011, about 26 percent of men and 22 percent of women in Canada claimed to have no religious affiliation. For those born between 1967 and 1986, for example, the rate was 29 percent. Comparatively, of Canada's oldest living generation, born in 1946 or earlier, only 12 percent claimed no religious affiliation.

INTERNET LINKS

www.naho.ca
The Native Aboriginal Health Organization has information about traditional healing.

www.pewforum.org/2013/06/27/canadas-changing-religious-landscape
The Pew Forum has an in-depth statistical overview of religion in Canada.

indigenousfoundations.arts.ubc.ca
This website, developed by the First Nations Studies Program of the University of British Columbia has information on government policy and the residential school system.

www.cbc.ca/history/EPCONTENTSE1EP2CH6PA2LE.html
"Biography: Marie de l'Incarnation," about Marie Guyard, is part of the website companion to the CBC television special *Canada, A People's History*.

BONNE FÊTE
du
LANGUAGE

CANADA

A French greeting card for Canada Day.

9

W ELCOME TO CANADA.
Bienvenue au Canada.

Tourists entering the country are always welcomed in both English and French. In fact, Canadians/Canadiens are accustomed to seeing English and French on all official forms, food packaging, street signs—in fact, just about everywhere.

There are some exceptions. The provinces have their own rules. In Alberta, one speaks English. *Au Québec, on parle français.* In Quebec, laws restrict the use of English on commercial signage. On the federal, or national level, however, Canadian laws accommodate both English and French as official languages of state. The Charter of Rights and Freedoms guarantees the right of the Canadian public to communicate in English and French with any central government office.

This doesn't mean all Canadians can speak both languages. In fact, the percentage of French-English bilingual Canadians is quite low—a mere 17.5 percent. Yet every Canadian has to study both languages in school.

Sociologists and statisticians divide the Canadian population into a spectrum of *francophones* (French speakers), *anglophones* (English speakers), and *allophones*. An allophone, a term used in Canada, is someone whose mother tongue is neither English nor French.

DIVIDED BY TONGUES

English and French were the languages of the original colonizers of the land. Today, the English-speaking community is distributed fairly evenly across Canada, while French-speaking Canadians are concentrated in the provinces of Quebec, New Brunswick, Ontario, and parts of Manitoba.

English is the mother tongue for most Canadians, except in Quebec,

Many indigenous languages in Canada are in danger of disappearing. Over the last century or so, at least ten flourishing aboriginal languages have gone extinct. Fewer than one in four aboriginal people can speak their ancestral language, and only 13 percent report speaking it at home.

where most are francophone, and in the north, where many First People speak their own languages. (One problem in assessing the language demographics of the country is that the word *allophone* refers to immigrants as well as to the indigenous people who speak their own languages. The First People, in particular, are peeved by this classification and resent being grouped with immigrants.)

BY THE NUMBERS

The proportion of Canadians who cite English as their mother tongue has been decreasing. From 1981 to 2006, the anglophone share of the total population declined from 61 percent to 58 percent. Of a total Canadian population of about 33 million, the 2011 census found the number of anglophone to be about 25 million and the francophone numbers to be about 7.5 million. The number of allophones was about 6.6 million. Since the allophone population is growing more rapidly than the English- or French-speaking population, experts predict the allophone population will soon overtake the francophone as the second-largest language demographic in Canada. The largest single non-official language spoken is Chinese, with more than 1 million speakers. Spanish, Italian, German, and Punjabi (mostly Pakistani) all come next with around 400,000 speakers each. Arabic speakers number more than 300,000.

CANADIAN ENGLISH

English is the second-most widely spoken language in the world. However, depending on where in the world it is being spoken, it can sound very different. Canadians, too, have their own brand of English.

Canadian English reflects from both British and American influences while also being distinctively Canadian. Generations of immigrants from Britain are responsible for the British accents that are discernible in Canadian speech. Americans have also had great influence on Canadian English. Most of the differences that Americans notice in Canadian speech are due to the influence of the British, while British visitors notice many features common to both American and Canadian English in spoken and written forms.

Canadians are comfortable switching between British and American terms and phrases. Sometimes they use them interchangeably. And some are primarily Canadian. Here are a few examples:

British	Canadian	American
trainers	*runners*	sneakers/tennis shoes
jumper	*sweater*	*sweater*
postcode	*postal code*	*ZIP code*
car park	*parkade*	*parking garage*
macaroni cheese	*Kraft dinner*	*mac and cheese*
bedsit or flat	*bachelor (apartment)*	*studio apartment*
cash dispenser	*ABM or bank machine*	*ATM*
chips	fries or chips	*(French) fries*

Differences in pronunciation are more obvious. For example, Canadians pronounce *tomato*, *dance*, *half*, and *clerk* the same way Americans do, but they pronounce *been*, *lever*, *ration*, and the letter *Z* ("zed") like the British do.

Canadians do not always spell the way the British or Americans do either. Canadian spelling contains a mixture of British and American spellings. It uses British spelling for many words, such as *behaviour*, *centre*, and *axe* (the American is *behavior*, *center*, and *ax*), and American spelling for some other words, such as *program*, *sulfur*, and *authorize* (as opposed to the British *programme*, *sulphur*, and *authorise*).

The almost uninterrupted flow of books and magazines, radio and television programs, and movies from south of the border and the movement and interaction of people in both directions have given American English an increasing influence on Canadian speech, especially among the nation's youth.

CANADIEN FRENCH

French speakers call themselves *Canadiens*, not Canadians. French as spoken in Canada is not a *patois* (dialect), nor a *creole* mixture of French, English, and an indigenous language. It is authentic French, brought to the country by the fewer than 10,000 original colonists who settled in New France in the seventeenth century. At that time, the French who came spoke various dialects, depending on their birthplace, but by the time the British took over the country with the Treaty of Paris in 1763, a Canadian brand of French had developed and had become the common language of the immigrants.

Cut off from their homeland, French Canadians developed a distinctly different language from that spoken in France. Increasingly under siege by a growing number of English-speaking newcomers, French Canadians resisted outside influence and developed a fierce pride that made them cling to their culture and language.

In some ways, Canadiens say their French is more French than Parisian French (which is considered the gold standard in France). In France, for example, stop signs say *STOP*, but in Québec, the signs say *ARRET*, which is the French word meaning *stop*. *Le week-end* in France is known as *la fin de semaine* ("the end of the week") in Québec. In France, a person sends "email," but in francophone Canada, one sends *courriel*.

Today, French universities in Quebec do considerable research into the French language, and l'Académie Canadienne-Française, l'Office de la Langue Française, and le Ministère d'Affaires Culturelles are entrusted with the task of ensuring that Canadian French continues to flourish in the country.

INDIGENOUS LANGUAGES

Anthropologists and linguists have classified the languages spoken by the indigenous peoples of Canada into eleven language families: Algonkian,

Athapaskan, Iroquoian, Siouan, Kutenaian, Salishan, Wakashan, Tsimshian, Haida, Tlingit, and Eskimo-Aleut. The eleven families together consist of around fifty-three individual languages. Indigenous peoples belonging to the same language family do not necessarily share the same culture. For example, the Blackfoot of the Plains and the Mi'kmaq of the Maritimes share a language that belongs to the Algonkian family, but their cultures are very different.

Of the indigenous languages that are still spoken in Canada, only three are widely used: Cree (Algonkian), Ojibway (Algonkian), and Inuktitut (Eskimo-Aleut). The others are in decline. In 2006, census statistics showed that 69 percent of Inuit, 29 percent of First Nations people, and 4 percent of Métis were able to converse in an Aboriginal language. Fortunately there is an increasing interest among the indigenous peoples themselves to try to preserve what remains by teaching their languages to their younger generations. The Northwest Territories government has encouraged the use of indigenous languages by adding six indigenous languages to its list of official languages.

INTERNET LINKS

www12.statcan.gc.ca
Statistics Canada. Select "Browse by subject," and then "Languages" for the latest census information.

www.noslangues-ourlanguages.gc.ca/index-eng.php
Language Portal of Canada has resources and tools on all aspects of English and French.

www.noslangues-ourlanguages.gc.ca/decouvrir-discover/langue-language/autochtones-aboriginal-eng.html
Same site as above with portal to aboriginal languages.

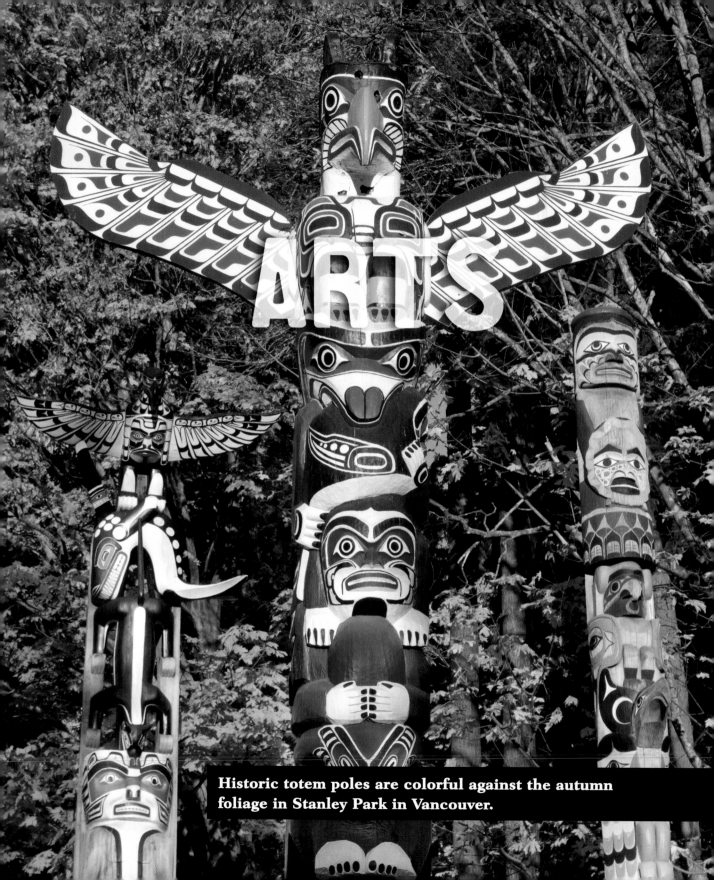

ARTS

Historic totem poles are colorful against the autumn foliage in Stanley Park in Vancouver.

10

THE HEART AND SOUL OF CANADA can be found in its arts—its music is the lapping of the waves against the hull of a fishing boat; its colors are the deep greens of forest pines and the red and white of its maple leaf flag; its poetry is the whisper of fog-bound mountains, or the cheering crowds at a hockey game. But of course, it's much more than that.

"Look at that sea, girls – all silver and shadow and vision of things not seen. We couldn't enjoy its loveliness any more if we had millions of dollars and ropes of diamonds."
   –Lucy Maud Montgomery, *Anne of Green Gables*

A whimsical spider sculpture perches in a plaza outside the National Gallery of Canada in Ottawa.

A HERITAGE CARVED IN WOOD

Totem poles are a distinctive sculptural art form of the Pacific Coast peoples, a tradition that dates back centuries. Back then, the tribes—including the Haida [HIGH-dah], Tlingit [KLIN-kit], and Tsimshian [SIM-she-an]—had no written language, but they had important information that they wanted to pass on through the generations. This they did by telling stories, a custom called oral tradition. And they recorded or illustrated those stories by making totem poles.

Spirits first taught the people to carve their stories into tall tree trunks, the stories say. Western red cedar was often the tree of choice because its wood is straight, abundant, and easy to carve. The powerful animals and fierce faces are not just decorations; they are symbols which represent legendary ancestors. The killer whale, raven, wolf, grizzly, hawk, beaver, and thunderbird, a mythological creature, all have special significance. Some poles honored the dead; others celebrated a birth or wedding. A pole outside the house of an important or wealthy person displayed the proud family history for all to see.

The symbolic meanings can differ from one tribe to the next, but they all celebrate the close— and even mystical—bond between the people and their natural environment. The figures on the poles aren't just any animals; they are creatures of the Pacific Coast region. The animals represent the land, life, and spirit of the people.

The art of totem pole carving almost died out during the last century when the indigenous people were forced to give up the old ways. But today those attitudes have changed and tribal craftsmen are happily reviving their culture using traditional methods and hand tools. When a pole is finished and ready to be raised, the people gather for a special ceremony of drumming, singing, and dancing.

Canadian arts reflect the diverse heritage of the nation's peoples. Where once it conveyed only the artistic perspective of the European colonizers, the Canadian arts scene has come to embrace the nation's indigenous cultures. The influence of the first peoples is seen and felt in many forms of contemporary Canadian art, from paintings to books to film. It appears that Canadian culture has returned to its roots in search of a way forward. At the same time, Canadians' growing pride in themselves and their achievements is reflected by a similar increase in uniquely Canadian art, literature, music, dramas, and movies.

INDIGENOUS ART

The indigenous arts existed in Canada centuries before the arrival of the Europeans. When the Europeans came, they influenced the development of the indigenous arts. For example, metal tools made it possible for indigenous artists, especially among the Inuit and peoples on the West Coast, to create more carved artifacts.

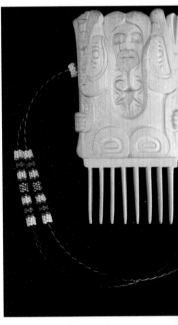

A delicately carved wooden comb is an example of the art of the Pacific Coast people.

The arts were very much a part of daily life. Song, dance, and mime were used to summon the spirits for guidance and predictions of the future. Figures carved from bone, stone, or wood were thought to have magical qualities and helped to relay ancestral stories to the young. Pottery, basketry, and weaving produced everyday items, while drums were used in religious ceremonies.

CANADIAN PAINTING

Early Canadian paintings were often romanticized depictions of Canadian life and land. Thomas Davies presented the beholder with pleasing and vivid but unrealistic watercolors of the Canadian landscape, while Paul Kane, who traveled from east to west to study and record the indigenous cultures, painted canvases that portrayed the native peoples in an idealized and heroic manner.

Toward the end of the nineteenth century, Ozias Leduc of Quebec and James Wilson Morrice of Montreal began to paint a distinctively Canadian landscape and lifestyle as they actually saw it. After their experiments came

"Hunting Salmon at Kettle Falls on Columbia River" is a painting by Paul Kane, a 19th century Canadian artist.

the works of Canada's most famous school of artists, the Group of Seven. They were Lawren Harris, A. Y. Jackson, Arthur Lismer, Frederick Varley, Franklin Carmichael, Frank (Franz) Johnston, and J.E.H. MacDonald. These painters were inspired by the works of fellow Canadian Tom Thomson, an artist and outdoorsman. Nature was their theme, and they recorded the forms and colors of the northern Ontario landscape as never done before—brutal, rugged landscapes, rocks fractured and cracked by frost, trees blasted by fierce storms, and villages clinging to gullied slopes.

In the 1930s, a group of French-Canadian painters, including Alfred Pellan, Paul-Emile Borduas, Jacques de Tonnancour, and Jean-Paul Riopelle, painted in the modernist experimental style that was the trend in the art centers of Paris and New York.

Paintings by David Milne and Emily Carr are also considered Canadian classics. Carr, a West Coast artist, depicted the great forests of giant cedar and fir and was greatly influenced by the art of the indigenous peoples of the West Coast. She became the first woman artist to achieve fame in

Canadian art. Later Canadian artists of note are Jack Shadbolt, another painter from western Canada who was similarly influenced by images of West Coast First Nations, and Robert Bateman, a painter and celebrator of Canadian wildlife.

CANADIAN WRITERS

Early Canadian writers used a descriptive style and told stories of Canadian life. For example, sisters Susanna Moodie and Catharine Parr Traill, who came from a comfortable life in nineteenth-century England to a harsh one in the Canadian bush, described the hardships of their pioneer experience. Stephen Leacock's *Sunshine Sketches of a Little Town* (1912) was an ironic, humorous look at small-town Ontario provincial life. But the Canadian novelist who truly captured the world's heart is Lucy Maud Montgomery, with her tales of an orphan girl on Prince Edward Island named Anne Shirley.

One of Canada's best-known authors, Margaret Atwood, holds one of her novels at a book festival in 2013.

Modern Canadian writers who have achieved worldwide fame include Ethel Wilson, Hugh MacLennan, Margaret Laurence, Mordecai Richler, Robertson Davies, Morley Callaghan, and singer-songwriter and poet Leonard Cohen.

The prolific Margaret Atwood, one of Canada's most popular authors, is especially well known for *The Handmaid's Tale* (1985), *Cat's Eye* (1988), and *The Blind Assassin* (2000) for which she won the prestigious Man Booker Prize. Yann Martel's novel *Life of Pi* (2001) won the Man Booker Prize and was made into a movie in 2012. Short story writer Alice Munro won the Nobel Prize for Literature in 2013.

Some indigenous Canadian writers of note are Maria Campbell, Thomson Highway, Beatrice Culleton, Daniel David Moses, Jeannette Armstrong, Ruby Slipperjack, and Basil Johnston.

CANADA IN VERSE In the 1890s, Canadian confederation was received with enthusiasm by the Confederation Poets, such as Bliss Carman, Charles Roberts, Archibald Lampman, and Duncan Campbell Scott. Roberts and

ANNE OF GREEN GABLES

When the young orphan girl Anne Shirley arrives in Avonlea on Prince Edward Island, she is excited at the prospect of being adopted by the middle-aged brother and sister, Matthew and Marilla Cuthbert. They live in a farmhouse called Green Gables and had requested an orphan to help with the farm work. But Anne quickly discovers that a mistake has been made. The Cuthberts had requested a boy, and taciturn Marilla is determined to send back the talkative, red-headed child.

That's the opening scene of Lucy Maud Montgomery's classic, Anne of Green Gables. *Published in 1908, the novel about the spunky, clever, and wildly imaginative girl was the first in a series of six Anne books. They have been read by generations of fans worldwide and are still very popular today. Each year, tourists flock to Cavendish, PEI, the inspiration for the fictional town of Avonlea to visit the real Green Gables farmhouse and a nearby Avonlea theme park.*

Anne of Green Gables *has been made into movies, TV series, a musical theater production, and was even adapted into Japanese anime. In fact, Anne is extraordinarily popular in Japan, where she is called* Akage no An, *or "Red-Haired Anne."*

Lampman wrote about rural life in the Maritime Provinces and Ontario. Scott observed the northern indigenous peoples.

In 1915, John McCrae of Guelph, Ontario, was serving as a surgeon in the Canadian Army when he wrote what is probably the most famous World War I poem, "In Flanders Fields." In the 1930s, E. J. Pratt, A.J.M. Smith, F. R. Scott, and A. M. Klein expressed Canadian ideals and aspirations. One of Smith's best-known poems, "The Lonely Land," (1936) celebrates the rugged, rocky, and wind-torn Canadian Shield. Pratt wrote epics on historic themes. Scott and Klein took a broad humanistic and cosmopolitan view of Canada and the world.

Canada's modern poets include Michael Ondaatje, Phyllis Webb, Margaret Atwood, Leonard Cohen, and Alden Nowlan. Ondaatje in particular rose to fame when he won the British Booker Prize in 1992 for his novel *The English Patient*.

PERFORMING ARTS

The film industry has become a valuable sector of the Canadian economy, especially in the two major film-making centers, Vancouver and Toronto. Canada's film industry brings in more than $5 billion in revenue each year. Low costs and the versatility of transforming Vancouver and Toronto into American settings are reasons for the popularity of the two cities.

Most Canadian cities have small theaters that present the works of Canadian playwrights. The Canada Council for the Arts gives grants to theaters, opera and dance companies, orchestras, and arts councils in the various municipalities to help promote and support their activities. In the 1970s, hundreds of new Canadian plays were written, after the Canada Council insisted that at least half of the productions performed in Canadian theaters had to feature local content.

Hip hop artist Drake performs at the Indiana State Fair in 2010.

The Canadian music industry grew from a base of folk songs, dance tunes, and religious and patriotic music. Canadian singers and songwriters were major factors in the popularity of folk music in the 1960s. The 1970s and 1980s saw the rise of many Canadian rock groups, and Canadian artists are well represented in the twenty-first century as well.

Some Canadian musicians and groups of note are Joni Mitchell, Neil Young, Gordon Lightfoot, Avril Lavigne, Justin Bieber, Barenaked Ladies, Celine Dion, Nelly Furtado, The Tragically Hip, Arcade Fire, Nickelback, Drake, Michael Bublé, k.d. lang, and David Usher.

Symphony orchestras and dance companies can be found in almost every city. The annual Shakespeare Festival at Stratford, Ontario, and the

Martin Short hosts the 2013 Canadian Screen Awards in Toronto.

Shaw Festival at Niagara-on-the-Lake, Ontario, are international events. Smaller towns and cities organize smaller-scale arts events. People often get together and form their own choral, symphonic, and theatrical groups.

A NATIONAL IMAGE

Two media organizations that have done much to cultivate and present Canadian culture are the Canadian Broadcasting Corporation (CBC) and the National Film Board (NFB). The CBC is Canada's national radio and television service. It began as a Crown corporation, or government company, in 1936, inspired partly by the example of the British Broadcasting Corporation.

The CBC was also an attempt to counter the growing U.S. influence on Canadian radio. The CBC seeks to bring Canadians closer together by building stronger bonds between various communities through its programs. It provides news of national and international importance, as well as light and educational programs.

John Grierson, a Scotsman, founded the NFB just before World War II. He had the task of creating a film company that could "interpret Canada to Canadians." The NFB nurtures emerging filmmakers and encourages innovative, creative productions. It has made many award-winning films and documentaries, teaching Canadians about their country.

THE CANADIAN SCREEN AWARDS

The first Canadian Film Awards were presented in 1949 in Ottawa. The idea behind the awards was to promote Canadian artists and raise film standards. The last awards were given in 1978; in 1979, the Academy of Canadian Cinema was formed to continue this work. The academy presented what were called the Genie Awards in more than twenty categories. In 2012 the Genie Awards became the Canadian Screen Awards. In 2014 the Academy of Canadian Cinema & Television celebrated sixty-five years of Canada's film industry.

The Canada Council for the Arts was created in 1957. Its function is to "foster and promote the study and enjoyment, and the production of works in, the arts." In order to do this, it gives grants to artists, organizations, and professional associations to help them in their cultural activities.

INTERNET LINKS

indigenousfoundations.arts.ubc.ca/home/culture/totem-poles.html
The University of British Columbia presents information about totem poles and links to other resources.

www.academy.ca/Canadian-Screen-Awards
The official site of the Academy of Canadian Cinema and Television lists the latest nominees and winners.

anne.sullivanmovies.com
This official Anne of Green Gables site focuses on the films made from the books.

www.gov.pe.ca/infopei/index.php3?number=2081
The Prince Edward Island site offers info about Lucy Maud Montgomery and the *Anne of Green Gables* books and local attractions.

www.goodreads.com/shelf/show/canadian-authors
Goodreads lists popular books by Canadian authors.

www.artcyclopedia.com/nationalities/Canadian.html
Artcyclopedia lists Canadian artists chronologically with many links.

Many TV and film stars are Canadians, even though they may work in the United States. Here are just a few:

Dan Ackroyd
Will Arnett
Jim Carrey
Michael Cera
Michael J. Fox
Ryan Gosling
Howie Mandel
Rachel McAdams
Rick Moranis
Sandra Oh
Ellen Page
Anna Paquin
Keanu Reeves
Ryan Reynolds
Seth Rogen
William Shatner
Donald Sutherland
Alex Trebeck

LEISURE

A young hockey fan learns to play the game.

THE AVERAGE CANADIAN WORKS five days, thirty-five to forty hours a week, and gets at least two weeks' paid vacation and nine public holidays a year. It has been estimated that the average Canadian enjoys a minimum of 124 leisure days a year; many enjoy more.

Canadians spend a good deal of their leisure time in the outdoors, enjoying the natural beauty of their country. However, they also watch a lot of television, especially sports programs, and spend an average of thirty hours a week in front of the TV. Time spent online is more or less comparable. Playing sports offers a break from all that sitting.

SPORTS

Canadians are sports enthusiasts. There is a sport for almost any kind of weather, at any temperature, from 85°F (29°C) in summer to 20°F (7°C) in winter. Many Canadian sports activities, such as tobogganing, snowshoeing, lacrosse, and canoeing, were introduced by the indigenous peoples. Canadians like other spectator sports, too. Here is a rundown:

LACROSSE This is the oldest Canadian game that is still played today. It was derived from a game called *baggataway*, which was played by the indigenous peoples as a means to develop group discipline and personal ingenuity.

 When the French came to Canada, they liked the game so much that they developed it into lacrosse. The first lacrosse club was formed

A PASSION FOR HOCKEY

In Canada, hockey is more than a game. It has been called a "unifying force" in a country that is often split by politics and language. Hockey is a symbol of Canadian identity itself.

The game was invented by a group of Canadian soldiers in Kingston, Ontario, on a winter day in 1855. To relieve the monotony of garrison duty, the soldiers tied blades to their boots and hit an old lacrosse ball using field hockey sticks.

Today, watching a hockey game has almost become a ritual. "Hockey Night in Canada" is the country's longest-running TV program—first airing in 1952.

Canadian teams such as the Montreal Canadiens, the Edmonton Oilers, the Toronto Maple Leafs, and the Vancouver Canucks, as well as U.S. teams such as the Chicago Blackhawks and the Detroit Red Wings, are members of the NHL. In the NHL Hall of Fame are Canadians Maurice "Rocket" Richard, Bobby Orr, Bobby Hull, and Wayne Gretzky, also known as the Great One. Gretzky played for the Edmonton Oilers and the Los Angeles Kings before retiring in 1999 and is considered the greatest hockey player of all time.

Canadians learn to love hockey from a very early age. The moment school is out, bags are tossed aside and goal posts set up in the neighborhood cul de sac, where half a dozen kids or so clash with hockey sticks to put an old tennis ball into the net. In the winter, the game is played on a frozen pond, stream, or indoor ice rink. Canadian children often dream of becoming stars in the National Hockey League (NHL). Parents devote hours of their time taking aspiring NHL players to and from games and practices.

At the Vancouver Olympics in 2010, Canadians rejoiced when both the men's and the women's Olympic hockey teams won gold medals. And in 2014, at the Winter Olympics in Sochi, history repeated itself when the Canadian men's (right) and women's teams once again brought home the gold.

in Montreal in 1839. In 1867 the game became so popular that the National Lacrosse Association of Canada was formed, the first national sports organization in the country.

BASEBALL is an American game that has captured a large Canadian following. Baseball diamonds are a necessary feature of playgrounds and parks in Canadian towns and cities. The game has been played in Canada professionally for more than a century. However, only one Canadian professional team, the Toronto Blue Jays, competes in Major League Baseball. (In 2004, the other Canadian team, the Montreal Expos, relocated to Washington, D.C. becoming the Washington Nationals.) In 1992 and 1993, the Blue Jays won back-to-back World Series championships, but haven't made it to the playoffs since. The Toronto SkyDome, now called the Rogers Centre, is the home of the Blue Jays. It was built in 1989 and has a retractable roof that covers the stadium when the weather gets bad.

Football, Canadian style: the Saskatchewan Roughriders play the Edmonton Eskimoes.

CANADIAN FOOTBALL   Canada played a role in the development of American football. It started out as a game similar to the British game of rugby, which was brought to Canada by immigrants. In 1874, players from McGill University traveled to Cambridge, Mass., to play against a Harvard team. When the McGill team arrived in Cambridge, the two teams realized they played different games with different rules and even different balls. Harvard played what it called "the Boston game," something more like soccer.

To solve the problem, the teams played two games, each under the other's rules. The Harvard team liked the Canadian version so much that they introduced it to other teams in the United States. American football players soon introduced their own rules, thus creating American football.

Canadian football today has a slightly different set of rules from American football, and the game is played on a larger field, with twelve players a side instead of eleven.

Football is played in high schools and colleges, but it is most popular in the big universities. The Canadian Football League (CFL) is the equivalent of the National Football League (NFL) in the United States. All the major cities in Canada have their own professional football teams, such as the Calgary Stampeders, the Ottawa Renegades, the Winnipeg Blue Bombers, the Edmonton Eskimos, and the BC Lions. American players are also allowed to play on Canadian teams.

BASKETBALL Created in 1891 by Canadian James Naismith, basketball has come to be a major part of the Canadian sports scene. Nearly every primary and secondary school in Canada has at least one basketball team, as do all of Canada's postsecondary institutions. Basketball courts can be found in many playgrounds and in most community centers. However, Canada has only one team in the National Basketball Association (NBA), the Toronto Raptors, since the Vancouver Grizzlies moved to Memphis, Tennessee, in 2001. The Raptors' home court is at the Air Canada Centre. The team won the Atlantic Division Championship in 2014.

GETTING OUTSIDE

For many Canadians, the wilderness is literally just outside the door. People who live in rural areas, or even in the suburbs of big cities, have access to parks and forests that are little more than minutes away. It is perhaps this proximity to nature that has made Canadians such an outdoorsy people.

During the summer months, city dwellers migrate where possible to cottages, parks, and resorts scattered across the vast network of lakes and rivers for which Canada is justly famous. Canoeing, boating, hiking, and camping are popular from coast to coast.

Hunting and fishing are also popular activities all year round, but a license has to be obtained first. Hunters shoot many types of game, from small birds, such as grouse and ducks, to big animals, such as deer, bear, and moose. But there are special seasons for certain kinds of game and a limit to the number that a hunter can shoot. Sport fishing is enjoyed on inland lakes and rivers as well as on the ocean. Ice fishing is also a popular winter pastime. Trout, salmon, and pike are among the catches.

Skiing is almost the natural thing to do. Winters are long and snowy. Downhill ski resorts in the mountainous Western Cordillera of British Columbia and Alberta, and the Laurentian Highlands of Quebec, north of Montreal and Quebec City, are world famous. British Columbia's renowned Whistler Blackcomb ski resort hosted many events in the 2010 Vancouver Winter Olympics.

Mont Tremblant in Quebec is one of Canada's most popular ski resorts.

INTERNET LINKS

www.pc.gc.ca
Parks Canada presents information about its national and provincial parks.

whc.unesco.org/en/list
UNESCO's interactive map of World Heritage sites.

www.tsn.ca
The Sports Network (TSN) is a Canadian English language sports channel. The site covers the NHL, NBA, MLB, CFL, NFL, and news of many other sports including curling and figure skating.

www.canadianliving.com
The website of *Canadian Living*, a lifestyle magazine.

FESTIVALS

Fireworks light the sky for Canada Day, July 1.

12

CANADIANS HAVE PLENTY TO celebrate and a wealth of ways to observe, honor, commemorate, remember, feast, make merry, or just plain have fun. On any day, somewhere in Canada, a festival or special event of some kind is bound to be taking place. It may be a celebration Canada shares with other countries, such as Christmas. Or it may be a Canadian event known all over the world, such as the Calgary Stampede.

Cowgirls gallop on horseback at the Calgary Stampede Parade in Alberta.

Since Canada claims the territory of the North Pole, many Canadian children are taught that Santa lives in Canada. The Canadian post office promotes this idea by promoting a "write to Santa" program that gives the jolly old elf a Canadian address and postal code.

THE MAJOR CHRISTIAN HOLIDAYS

Canada is a predominantly Christian country. Christmas and Easter are celebrated in much the same way they are in the United States and other countries. For religious people, these are important holy days that commemorate the birth of Jesus at Christmas and his resurrection from the dead at Easter time. Church services are an important part of these holidays, which also include the familiar rituals and family meals.

These holidays also have a secular side, corresponding as they do to the winter solstice and return of life during the spring time. Santa Claus and the Easter Bunny are beloved symbols of the holidays in Canada just as they are elsewhere, for the religious and secular-minded alike.

THANKSGIVING

Harvest time is a time of thanksgiving in Canada. Although people are becoming more removed from the land, they continue the tradition of giving thanks for a good harvest. In Canada, Thanksgiving falls on the second Monday of October, earlier than in the United States, where Thanksgiving is the fourth Thursday of November and is closely connected to the history of the Pilgrims.

Despite differences in date and reason, Canadians and Americans celebrate Thanksgiving in much the same way. Family members come home to be with one another and enjoy a Thanksgiving dinner of roast turkey with cranberry sauce, stuffing, potatoes, green vegetables, and a pumpkin pie for dessert.

REMEMBRANCE DAY

On Remembrance Day, Canadians call to mind those who died while fighting in the two world wars and the Korean War. Canadians celebrate Remembrance Day, known as Veterans' Day in the United States, on November 11. The armistice that officially ended World War I took effect at the eleventh hour of the eleventh day of the eleventh month—that is, at 11 a.m. on November 11—in 1918.

On Remembrance Day, Canadians hold special ceremonies in towns and cities. Members of the Royal Canadian Legion, with other uniformed groups and service clubs, gather to honor and respect those who died serving the country. The Remembrance Day ceremony usually includes a recitation of "In Flanders Fields," a poem by Colonel John McCrae of Guelph, Ontario.

CANADA DAY

Canada Day, formerly called Dominion Day, is celebrated on July 1, the anniversary of the creation of the Dominion of Canada in 1867. Towns and cities all over the country hold their own ceremonies on Canada Day to celebrate the unity of the country. The capital, Ottawa, hosts a large annual celebration that attracts Canadians from across the country. The year 2017 will be special for Canadians, because it will mark the 150th birthday of the country.

A war veteran carries the Canadian flag during the 2013 Remembrance Day ceremonies in Abbotsford, British Columbia.

CELEBRATING ORIGINS

Canadians come from diverse backgrounds. The multicultural character of society can be seen in the way people of different origins, religions, and traditions continue to celebrate these differences.

Long before the Europeans came to Canada, the indigenous peoples marked the year with festivals celebrating the seasons or religious rituals. The Ojibway had thanks-giving rituals in spring to celebrate the end of winter and in the fall for the bountiful harvest.

The indigenous peoples of the West Coast held ceremonial feasts called *potlatches*, while those of the Plains held lively cultural gatherings called *powwows*. The word *powwow* comes from the old Algonquin word for "medicine man."

Today, powwows are inter-tribal gatherings that celebrate the rituals and spiritual beliefs of the indigenous peoples. The powwow is held over a number of days, during which there is almost nonstop singing, dancing, and drumming, and a continuous parade of traditional and ceremonial indigenous

THE POTLATCH

The potlatch was a type of festival held in Pacific Coast indigenous communities, in which a chief invited people to a celebration of feasting, dancing, and gift-giving. Potlatches were held to mark rites of initiation, to mourn the dead, or to celebrate the investiture of a new chief. During the ceremonies, native ancestral spirits were invoked, usually in a mythological animal form.

At the potlatch, which could last for days, the host chief presented gifts to his guests. The value of the gift corresponded directly to the guest's social ranking. The greater the

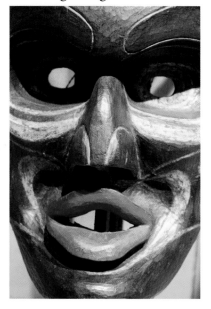

prestige of the chief, the more wealth he distributed in gifts. When his guests held their own potlatches, they were expected to give even more lavishly or they would be shamed. A chief who made himself poor by giving lavishly at a potlatch could count on having his wealth returned at subsequent potlatches where he would be a guest. These festivals of gift giving were not merely parties or religious rituals. They had political, religious, kinship, and economic implications for the extended communities.

The potlatch was important in establishing the status, rank, and privileges of the people. However, in the nineteenth century, government officials in both Canada and the United States suspected the potlatch ceremonies of promoting non-Christian values. They thought the custom empowered the Indian people and undermined the authority of the federal government, so they banned the practice altogether. In so doing, the laws helped to destroy indigenous culture, which of course was the true goal.

The ban was finally lifted in 1934 in the United States and in 1951 in Canada. Potlatches are once again being held today but never on the same scale as in the past.

dress and arts and crafts. Like the healing ceremonies performed by medicine men of the past, the powwow is a healing and unifying ritual that enables the indigenous peoples to show their pride in their culture.

The oldest European immigrant groups hold festivals that display their foods, handicrafts, and lifestyles. The Festival du Voyageur in Saint Boniface,

Winnipeg's French Quarter, celebrates the *joie de vivre*, or joy of life, of the region's early fur traders. In winter, Quebecers enjoy themselves at le Carnaval de Quebec. Scots-Canadians celebrate the annual Highland Games at Antigonish, Nova Scotia, and gather every four years in Nova Scotia for the International Gathering of the Clans.

Ukrainians in the town of Dauphin, Manitoba, hold a National Ukrainian Festival, which showcases Ukrainian costumes, artifacts, and fiddling contests. The Vesna Festival, in Saskatoon, Saskatchewan, is another Ukrainian festival of foods and handicrafts. The Pioneer Days Parade in Steinbach, Manitoba, celebrates Mennonite heritage with a display of threshing, baking, and food samples. The large Chinese community in Vancouver, British Columbia, celebrates the Chinese New Year with dragon dances and firecrackers.

In the Rocky Mountains of Alberta, Blackfoot people are in traditional dress for a powwow.

INTERNET LINKS

canada150.gc.ca
Canada 150 marks yearly milestones leading up to the 150th anniversary of confederation.

www.neverstoptraveling.com/great-canadian-summer-festivals
A comprehensive list, with links, of Canadian summer festivals.

www.2camels.com/festivals/canada.php
This site lists year-round festivals by type, time, and location.

firstpeoplesofcanada.com/fp_groups/fp_nwc5.html
The First Peoples of Canada site has a colorful, photo-rich section on the Northwest Coastal People, which includes information about the potlatch as well as other aspects of the culture.

FOOD

A droplet of maple sap flows from the tree into a pail. It will be boiled down into pure maple syrup, one of Canada's most iconic foods.

13

CANADIAN FOOD DOESN'T USUALLY top the list of the world's greatest cuisines. Generally, it has a basic meat and potatoes theme to it—an amalgam of British, American, and no-frills French home cooking, with some First Nations influence thrown in. At least that's the usual perception. In truth, however, Canadian cookery ranges from the haute cuisine of top restaurants, to every kind of fast food, to a wide variety of ethnic specialties, to some particularly—some might say peculiarly—Canadian fare.

Seal flipper pie, poutine, Montreal smoked meat, tourtiere, Nanaimo bars, butter tarts, beaver tails (fried dough with cinnamon sugar topping), and schmoo torte are just some of the distinctively Canadian dishes. And of course, anything made with maple syrup.

THE BOUNTY OF THE SEA

In the Atlantic provinces of Newfoundland, Prince Edward Island, Nova Scotia, and New Brunswick, fish—especially cod—is available year round. It may be fresh, dried, pickled, or salted, and then cooked in a variety of ways.

A fisherman pulls a big pike from under the ice.

In Newfoundland, seal flipper pie is a specialty. To make it, the cook has to scrape off the hair and cut off the blubber from seal's flippers, simmer the flippers for a long time, add pork and flour to make a stew-like mixture, and cover the mixture with pastry. Another popular dish of Newfoundlanders is boiled salted pork or beef with potatoes, turnips, carrots, and cabbage.

The food of Nova Scotia reflects the cuisines of the Scottish, English, German, Swiss, and French settlers in the province. Examples of Nova Scotia dishes are fish chowder, Lunenburg sausage with sauerkraut, and Solomon Gundy, a dish of cured herring fillets mixed with spices and onions. More recently, donair, a beef kabob with a sweet sauce, has become a Nova Scotian specialty.

New Brunswick is known for its clam chowder, made with the large clams of the Shediac region. Dulse is an edible seaweed that grows on the rocks in the North Atlantic and Northwest Pacific oceans, and is harvested along the shores of New Brunswick and Nova Scotia and of islands such as the Grand Manan. The oysters of Prince Edward Island's Malpeque Bay are used to make a rich soup called oyster bisque; and lobster, mussels, and potatoes are among PEI's other famous foods.

THE FRENCH CONNECTION

Everybody knows that the French and good food go together; the same applies to French-Canadians. Few would disagree that the two best cities in Canada for good French restaurants are Montreal and Quebec City. Many restaurants in these cities used to serve mainly fancy French food, or *haute cuisine*, such as *paté de foie gras* (an appetizer made of goose liver) or *coq au vin* (chicken simmered in Burgundy wine), but traditional French-Canadian country food has found its place on their menus too.

Inspired by home cooking, restaurants in Quebec now offer *tourtière*, a spiced meat pie that is traditionally served on Christmas Eve, maple sugar pie, *cretons*, a meat spread for sandwiches, and Oka cheese, among other local dishes.

Quebec is also the origin of one of the most iconic Canadian dishes, *poutine*. Far from haute cuisine—and certainly not diet or health food—it's a favorite indulgence for many Canadians and tourists. Poutine is a plate of salty French fries topped with cheese curds and drenched in hot gravy. Cheese curds are a type of fresh white cheese with a squeaky consistency. Cheddar or mozzarella can apparently be substituted, but the results are not the same.

Cretons is a Quebec meat pate made with pork, onion, and spices. It is often served on toast for breakfast.

COSMOPOLITAN ONTARIO

Ontario, especially Toronto, is one of Canada's most cosmopolitan regions. Half of Toronto's residents were born outside the country. Immigrants have given the province a special flavor in terms of food, from solid English steak and kidneys to delicate Italian capellini.

The British preserved their love for creamed kippers and minced lamb pie even as they learned to appreciate more exotic foods. Italians, mainly from southern Italy, opened shops selling blocks of Parmesan cheese, bins full of olives, and vegetables such as artichokes and zucchini. Hungarians, Yugoslavs, Poles, and Rumanians added their own variations of dumplings, stews, and sauerkraut.

NORTH COUNTRY FOODS

Wild game forms a large part of the diet in the north, where people still hunt, fish, and trap for food. Country foods remain the staple diet of the northern indigenous peoples, partly because they are more economical than food sold in stores. Country foods are also recognized as being healthier than processed food.

The indigenous peoples traditionally hunt big animals such as moose and caribou in large groups. They share the meat in their families and communities

MAPLE SYRUP

To some people, maple syrup is synonymous with Canada. After all, the maple leaf is on the nation's flag. Quebec is by far the world's leading producer of maple syrup, and Ontario makes it as well.

Maple syrup is harvested in the early springtime, when the days are warm and the nights are cold. This is the time when the sap of the maple tree rises from the roots and runs through the tree.

The indigenous people of northeastern North America first figured out how to make syrup from sap and used it in their cooking. They in turn taught the Europeans, who added technological improvements to the collection and production methods. Mature maple trees are tapped by driving a spigot into the side of the tree. A bucket or plastic tube

is attached to the spigot to collect the sap, which is sweet but thin. In order to make just a gallon of syrup, about forty times more sap has to be collected. Another way of visualizing this is, about ten gallons of sap must be boiled down to make one quart of syrup.

The maple tree sap is put in special containers and boiled until it becomes sufficiently thick. Sugaring off, as the boiling process is called, is a great social event. Children in particular love it, because they get to enjoy a special treat called sugar on snow—chewy bits of toffee made by splashing some of the hot, thick maple syrup onto clean snow on the ground.

as a way of reinforcing kinship and bonds. Smaller game such as waterfowl and rabbits are hunted in smaller groups. Indigenous groups that live in the west fish for salmon, which is smoked and dried. Groups along the coast fish for arctic char and cod and hunt whales, seals, and walruses. Inuit also hunt polar bears for their hide, fat, and flesh.

In summer, indigenous peoples gather berries, blueberries probably being the most popular. They also gather root vegetables to supplement their diet. Indigenous peoples in some areas use wood chips from cedar, maple, and hickory trees, and even pine cones to flavor their food.

BRITISH COLUMBIA WITH AN ASIAN ACCENT

Chinese, Japanese, Indians, and other Asians form large minorities in the province of British Columbia, especially in Vancouver. They have added their foods to Canadian cuisine. Asian foods such as tofu, noodles, and curry, and spices such as cumin and cardamom can commonly be found on supermarket shelves in British Columbia.

British Columbia is also known for the variety and quality of its fish. There are five varieties of Pacific salmon: chum, coho, pink, sockeye, and chinook. Huge quantities of salmon are caught every year in the province. They reach the markets fresh, smoked, or canned. The abundance of salmon and other fish along the West Coast, together with the presence of many Asian-born residents and visitors, has made Vancouver one of the world's best locations for delicious and amazingly affordable sushi.

British Columbia produces a wealth of fruit, including peaches, pears, plums, melons, berries, and apples. Loganberries and giant Zucca melons are two special fruits seldom found anywhere outside the province. Loganberries, a cross between raspberries and blackberries, are cultivated on Vancouver Island.

INTERNET LINKS

allrecipes.com/recipes/world-cuisine/canadian
All Recipes has several Canadian food recipe collections

www.thecanadaguide.com/food
This is a cute, quick overview of iconic Canadian foods, including some commercial products.

www.macleans.ca/society/life/12-foods-canada-has-given-the-world-besides-poutine
This site offers another list of iconic Canadian foods.

EASY POUTINE

Poutine is very filling. It's a full meal in itself, not an appetizer or side dish. Serve it very hot for best results.

1 bag of frozen French fried potatoes (or make homemade fries according to your favorite recipe)
2 cups white cheddar cheese curds*
1 (10.25 ounce) can of beef gravy (or substitute mushroom or chicken gravy)
salt

Prepare the fries according to the package directions. Meanwhile, heat the gravy to a near simmer. Place hot fries into large rimmed platter or shallow bowl. Salt the fries, sprinkle with cheese. Drizzle with hot gravy. Serve immediately.

*Cheese curds—bite-size bits of very fresh cheese that "squeaks"—are commonly found in Quebec. They are not easy to find in the United States. If necessary, substitute small chunks of mozzarella, Monterey jack, or mild cheddar cheese. However, the result won't be quite the same.

CANADIAN BUTTER TARTS

Crust
1 and 1/2 cups all-purpose flour
1/4 tsp salt
1/4 cup cold butter, cubed
1/4 cup lard, cubed
1 egg yolk
1 tsp vinegar
Ice water

Filling
1/2 cup packed brown sugar
1/2 cup corn syrup
1 egg
2 tbsp butter, softened
1 tsp vanilla
1 tsp vinegar
1 pinch salt
1/4 cup currants, raisins, pecans, or shredded coconut

Crust: Preheat oven to 450° F. In large bowl, whisk flour with salt. With pastry blender, cut in butter and lard until crumbly. In a measuring cup, whisk egg yolk with vinegar; add enough ice water to make 1/3 cup. Sprinkle over flour mixture, stirring briskly with fork until pastry holds together. Press into disc; wrap in plastic wrap, and refrigerate about 1 hour (or up to 3 days) .

Filling: In bowl, whisk together brown sugar, corn syrup, egg, butter, vanilla, vinegar and salt until blended; set aside. On lightly floured surface, roll out pastry to 1/8-inch thickness. Using 4-inch round cookie cutter, cut out 12 circles, rerolling scraps once if necessary. Fit into muffin cups. Divide fruit or nuts among shells. Spoon in filling until three-quarters full.

Bake in bottom third of 450° F oven until filling is puffed and bubbly and pastry is golden, about 12 minutes. Let stand on rack for 1 minute. Run metal spatula around tarts to loosen; carefully slide spatula under tarts and transfer to rack to let cool. Makes 12 tarts.

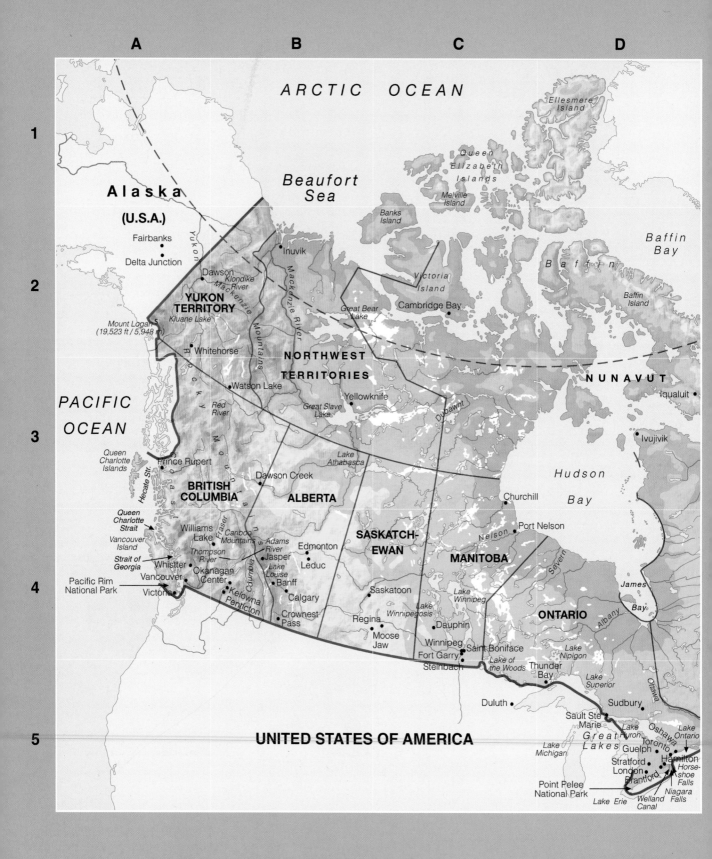

MAP OF CANADA

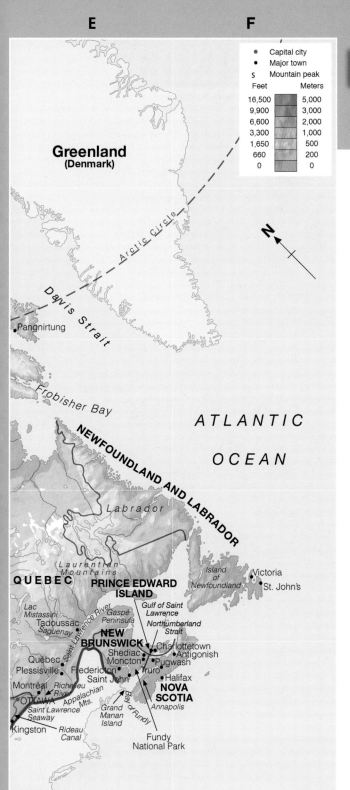

Capital city
Major town
Mountain peak

Feet		Meters
16,500		5,000
9,900		3,000
6,600		2,000
3,300		1,000
1,650		500
660		200
0		0

ECONOMIC CANADA

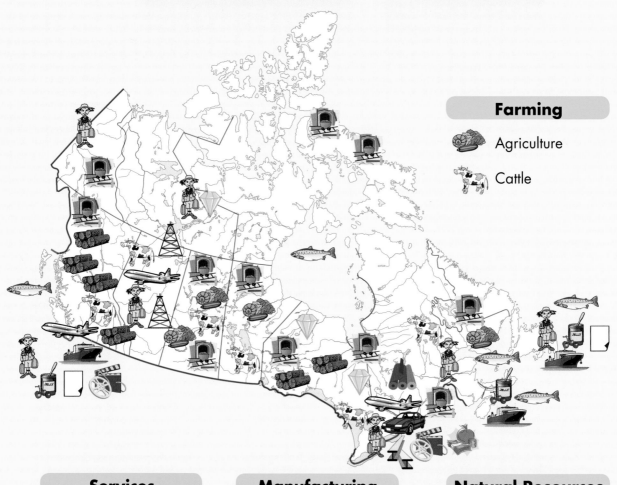

Farming

 Agriculture

Cattle

Services

Airport

Filmmaking

Finance

Port

Tourism

Manufacturing

Automobiles

Food Products

Pulp & Paper

Steel

Textiles

Natural Resources

Diamond

Fish

Forestry

Oil

Other Minerals

ABOUT THE ECONOMY

OVERVIEW

Canada is a high-tech industrial society with abundant natural resources and a highly skilled labor force. Canada exports about three-fourths of its merchandise to the United States. Canada is the United States' largest foreign supplier of energy, including oil, gas, uranium, and electric power. Alberta's oil sands have significantly boosted Canada's proven oil reserves. Canada now ranks third in the world in proved oil reserves behind Saudi Arabia and Venezuela.

GROSS DOMESTIC PRODUCT (GDP)

$1.518 trillion

CURRENCY

1 Canadian dollar (CAD) = 100 cents
Notes: 5, 10, 20, 50, 100, 1,000 dollars
Coins: 1, 5, 10, 25 cents; 1, 2 dollars
USD 1 = CAD 1.10 (April 2014)

GDP SECTORS

agriculture: 1.7 percent
industry: 28.4 percent
services: 69.9 percent (2013)

NATURAL RESOURCES

Iron ore, nickel, zinc, copper, gold, lead, rare earth elements, molybdenum, potash, diamonds, silver, fish, timber, wildlife, coal, petroleum, natural gas, hydropower

LAND AREA

3.9 million square miles (9,976,000 sq km)

INFLATION RATE

1 percent (2013)

WORKFORCE

19.08 million (2013)

WORKFORCE BY OCCUPATION

agriculture: 2 percent
manufacturing: 13 percent
construction: 6 percent
services: 76 percent
other: 3 percent (2006)

UNEMPLOYMENT RATE

7.1 percent (2013)

AGRICULTURAL PRODUCTS

Wheat, barley, oilseed, tobacco, fruits, vegetables; dairy products; fish; forest products

INDUSTRIAL PRODUCTS

transportation equipment, chemicals, processed and unprocessed minerals, food products, wood and paper products, fish products, petroleum and natural gas

MAJOR TRADE PARTNERS

The United States, China, United Kingdom, Mexico

MAJOR PORTS AND HARBORS

Vancouver, Toronto, Montreal, Halifax, Saint John's

CULTURAL CANADA

S. S. Klondike
Built in 1937, it was one of the last and largest sternwheelers used on the Yukon River. It made its last run upriver in 1955 and is now dry-docked in Whitehorse to serve as a museum and historic site.

Old Quebec City
First explored by Jacques Cartier in 1535, the city was founded by Samuel de Champlain in 1608. Two of North America's oldest streets—Rue Sous le Cap and Rue du Petit Champlain—are located here. The city is on the United Nations' World Heritage list.

L'Anse aux Meadows National Historic Park
Fronted by the Atlantic Ocean, this park in the north of western Newfoundland probably looks much the same as it did in 1000 CE to the Vikings—the first Europeans to land in North America. Vestiges of the original wood and sod buildings of the Vikings remain.

House of Green Gables
In Cavendish is the house made famous by Lucy Maud Montgomery's book, Anne of Green Gables. The story about a young orphan and her tribulations was set in Prince Edward Island at the turn of the 20th century.

Whistler-Blackcomb
One of North America's top ski resorts, where skiing is sometimes possible even in summer. Together with Vancouver city, Whistler-Blackcomb hosted the 2010 Winter Olympics.

Banff National Park
Established in 1885, Canada's first national park covers 2,564 square miles (6,641 square km). In addition to the hot springs that made it famous, Banff also offers skiing and climbing. But most visitors come just to walk the many trails and take in the stunning scenery of the Rockies.

Lower Fort Garry
North of Winnipeg on the banks of the Red River is a restored Hudson's Bay Company fort. It dates back to the 1830s and is the only stone fort still intact from the fur-trading days.

Niagara Falls
The Canadian Horseshoe Falls are particularly spectacular. Visitors can view the scene either from observation decks by the falls or bottom-up from the deck of ferries. Rock-cut tunnels provide for a closer (and wet) view of the falls from behind.

Bay of Fundy
The world's highest tides are in the south of New Brunswick. The contrast between the high and ebb tide is most pronounced at the eastern end of the bay and around the Minas Basin, where tides of 32–50 feet (10–15 m) occur twice daily about 12 and a half hours apart.

Fort Anne National Historic Site
In the city center of Annapolis Royal, Nova Scotia, this park showcases early Acadian settlement life and contains the remnants of the 1635 French fort, mounds and moats still intact.

ABOUT THE CULTURE

OFFICIAL NAME
Canada

CAPITAL
Ottawa

DESCRIPTION OF NATIONAL FLAG
Eleven-point red maple leaf on white, framed by red bars.

NATIONAL ANTHEM
"O Canada." Adopted July 1, 1980. (To listen, go to www.pch.gc.ca/progs/cpsc-ccsp/sc-cs/anthem_e.cfm)

OTHER MAJOR CITIES
Calgary, Edmonton, Montreal, Quebec City, Toronto, Vancouver, Victoria, Saskatoon, Regina, Winnipeg, Halifax, Saint John's

PROVINCES AND TERRITORIES
Alberta, British Columbia, Manitoba, New Brunswick, Newfoundland, Northwest Territories, Nova Scotia, Nunavut, Ontario, Prince Edward Island, Quebec, Saskatchewan, Yukon

GOVERNMENT
A parliamentary democracy, a federation, and a constitutional monarchy

POPULATION
34,834,841 (2014)

MAJOR ETHNIC GROUPS
Canadian 32.2 percent, English 19.8 percent, French 15.5 percent, Scottish 14.4 percent, Irish 13.8 percent, German 9.8 percent, Italian 4.5 percent, Chinese 4.5 percent, North American Indian 4.2 percent, other 50.9 percent (2011)

RELIGIOUS GROUPS
Roman Catholic, 38.7 percent; Protestant, 20.3 percent; other Christians, 6.3 percent; Muslim, 3.2 percent; Hindu, Sikh, Buddhist, Jewish, 5 percent; none, 23.9 percent (2011)

OFFICIAL LANGUAGES
English and French

LITERACY RATE
99 percent

HOLIDAYS New Year's Day (January 1), Good Friday and Easter (March/April), Canada Day (July 1), Thanksgiving (2nd Monday in October), Remembrance Day (November 11), Christmas (December 25)

LEADERS IN POLITICS
Stephen Harper, prime minister (2006—)
Paul Martin—prime minister (2003—2006)
Jean Chrétien—prime minister (1993—2003)

TIMELINE

IN CANADA	IN THE WORLD

10,000 BCE
Indigenous groups spread over Canada.

753 BCE
Rome is founded.

116–17 BCE
The Roman Empire reaches its greatest extent, under Emperor Trajan (98–17).

500 CE
Indigenous groups develop extensive social and economic links.

600 CE
Height of Mayan civilization

992
Leif Ericsson explores Newfoundland.

1000
The Chinese perfect gunpowder and begin to use it in warfare.

1534
Jacques Cartier discovers the Saint Lawrence River.

1492
Christopher Columbus sails to North America

1558–1603
Reign of Elizabeth I of England

1603
Samuel Champlain explores the Great Lakes.

1620
Pilgrims sail the *Mayflower* to America.

1632
Champlain is appointed the first governor.

1763
France recognizes British claims to Canada and cedes Nova Scotia.

1774
Quebec Act upholds French civil law.

1776
U.S. Declaration of Independence

1791
Upper and Lower Canada are created.

1789–99
The French Revolution

1841
Act of Union creates the Province of Canada.

1858
Ottawa is chosen as Canada's capital.

1861
The U.S. Civil War begins.

IN CANADA	IN THE WORLD
1867 Union of Canada	**1869** The Suez Canal opens.
1870–73 Northwest Territories, British Columbia, Manitoba, and Prince Edward Island join Canada.	
1903 Alaskan Panhandle becomes part of the U.S.	
1905 Alberta and Saskatchewan join Canada.	**1914** World War I begins.
1920 Canada joins the League of Nations.	**1939** World War II begins.
1949 Newfoundland joins Canada. Canada joins NATO.	**1949** The North Atlantic Treaty Organization (NATO) is formed.
	1957 The Russians launch Sputnik.
1960 Indigenous Canadians win the right to vote.	**1969** Apollo 11 lands on the moon; U.S. astronaut Neil Armstrong is first to walk on the moon.
	1991 Break-up of the Soviet Union
1995 Quebecois vote to remain part of Canada.	**1997** British return Hong Kong to China.
1999 The territory of Nunavut is created.	**2001** Terrorists crash planes in New York, Washington, D.C., and Pennsylvania.
	2003 War in Iraq
2006 Stephen Harper becomes prime minister	
2010 Vancouver hosts the Winter Olympics	
2013 Alice Munro is first Canadian woman to win Nobel Prize in Literature.	**2013** Prince George of Cambridge is born in England.

GLOSSARY

baggataway
An indigenous game played to develop group discipline and personal ingenuity.

Calgary Stampede
A famous Canadian festival of rodeos and races held every July in Calgary, Alberta.

Confederation
The union of New Brunswick, Nova Scotia, and the Province of Canada in 1867, forming the Dominion of Canada. Included the Northwest Territories in 1870, British Columbia in 1871, Prince Edward Island in 1873, Yukon in 1898, Newfoundland in 1949, and Nunavut in 1999.

Crown land
Canadian land belonging to the public and administered by the government.

First Nations
The name by which Canada's aboriginal peoples prefer to be known.

Inuit
An aboriginal people, previously called Eskimos, who inhabit the northern, Arctic areas of Canada and Greenland.

Maritimes
The collective name for the provinces of Prince Edward Island, Nova Scotia, and New Brunswick.

Mountie
An officer of the Royal Canadian Mounted Police.

New France
The name of French-controlled North America until 1763, encompassing a part of present-day United States and Canada.

potlatch
An indigenous ceremonial feast.

poutine
A dish of French fries, cheese curds, and hot gravy.

powwow
An indigenous cultural gathering or festival.

prairie
An open, grass-covered, treeless landscape. The Canadian prairies cover the southern parts of Alberta, Saskatchewan, and Manitoba.

shaman
A medicine man, a spiritual and bodily healer.

teepee
A tent made of animal skins stretched over a framework of poles.

territories
Federally governed regions with smaller populations than the provinces. Canada has three: Yukon, the Northwest Territories, and Nunavut.

Vikings
Seafaring people from Norway or other parts of Scandinavia who explored and attacked Northern Europe in eighth to tenth centuries

FOR FURTHER INFORMATION

BOOKS

Baird, Elizabeth, and Rose Murray. *Canada's Favourite Recipes*. North Vancouver: Whitecap Books, 2012.

DK Eyewitness Travel Guide: Canada. New York: DK Publishing, 2012.

Driver, Elizabeth. *The All New Purity Cookbook*. Vancouver: Whitecap Books, 2001.

Greenwood, Barbara. *The Kids Book of Canada*. Kids Can Press, 2007.

Hacker, Carlotta. *The Kids Book of Canadian History*. Kids Can Press, 2009.

Miller, J.R. *Skyscrapers Hide the Heavens, A History of White-Indian Relations in Canada*. Toronto: University of Toronto Press, 2000.

Noel, Jan. *Along a River: The First French-Canadian Women*. Toronto: University of Toronto Press, 2013.

Penn, Briony. *The Kids Book of Canadian Geography*. Kids Can Press, 2008.

Sellars, Bev. *They Called Me Number One: Secrets and Survival at an Indian Residential School*. Vancouver: Talonbooks, 2013.

DVDS/FILMS

Atanarjuat (The Fast Runner). Sony Pictures Home Entertainment, 2002.

Canada Explorer. Topics Entertainment, 2013.

The Great Canadian Train Ride: From Toronto to Vancouver. Total Content, 2005.

Great North. Razor, 2005.

NOVA — The Vikings. PBS, 2006.

Vikings: Journey to New Worlds. Vista Point Entertainment, 2006.

WEBSITES

Aboriginal Affairs and Northern Development Canada. www.aadnc-aandc.gc.ca

Canadian Geographic. www.canadiangeographic.ca

Canada.com. www.canada.com

Canada History. www.canadahistory.com

Canada's First Peoples. www.firstpeoplesofcanada.com

CBC News. www.cbc.ca

Government of Canada. www.gc.ca

Hockey Canada. www.hockeycanada.ca

Infoplease.com, Canada. www.infoplease.com/country/canada.html

Lonely Planet World Guide: Destination Canada. www.lonelyplanet.com/canada

National Gallery of Canada. www.gallery.ca

Statistics Canada. www.statcan.ca

BIBLIOGRAPHY

WEBSITES

Aboriginal Affairs and Northern Development Canada. www.aadnc-aandc.gc.ca

Canadahistory.com. www.canadahistory.com

Canadian Encyclopedia, The. www.thecanadianencyclopedia.com

Canadian Geographic. www.canadiangeographic.ca

Canadian Government. www.canada.ca

Canadian Heritage. www.pch.gc.ca

Canadian Museum of History. www.historymuseum.ca

Canadian Parliament. www.parl.gc.ca

CBC. "Canada: A People's History." www.cbc.ca/history/index.html

CBC News. "FAQs: The Atlantic seal hunt."
    www.cbc.ca/news/canada/faqs-the-atlantic-seal-hunt-1.803159

COSEWIC. www.cosewic.gc.ca

Environment Canada. www.ec.gc.ca

First Peoples of Canada. www.firstpeoplesofcanada.com

The Museum of Natural History (Smithsonian Institutes). "Vinland."
    www.mnh.si.edu/vikings/voyage/subset/vinland/archeo.html

Harp Seals.org. www.harpseals.org

Health Care Canada. www.hc-sc.gc.ca

Index Mundi. "United States vs. Canada."
    www.indexmundi.com/factbook/compare/united-states.canada/economy

Indigenous Foundations. http://indigenousfoundations.arts.ubc.ca

Language Portal of Canada. www.noslangues-ourlanguages.gc.ca/index-eng.php

Legatum Institute. www.prosperity.com

Native Aboriginal Health Organization. www.naho.ca

Nunavut Tourism. www.nunavuttourism.com

OECD Better Life Index. www.oecdbetterlifeindex.org/countries/canada

Parks Canada. www.pc.gc.ca

Pew Research Religion & Public Life Project. "Canada's Changing Religious Landscape."
    www.pewforum.org/2013/06/27/canadas-changing-religious-landscape

Royal Canadian Mounted Police. www.rcmp-grc.gc.ca

Sea Shepherd.org. www.seashepherd.org/seals/seal-hunt-facts.html

The Sports Network (TSN). www.tsn.ca

Statistics Canada. www12.statcan.gc.ca

UNESCO. Interactive map of World Heritage sites. whc.unesco.org/en/list

UNSDSN. www.unsdsn.org/resources/publications/world-happiness-report-2013

INDEX

INDEX